OUT *of the* WOODS

Environmental Timber Frame Design for Self Build

Acknowledgements

Pat Borer is an architect with his own practice in Mid-Wales. He has been involved with the Centre for Alternative Technology since early days and has helped evolve the ecological self build approach to design apparent in the Centre's buildings. He is an advisor to the Walter Segal Self Build Trust.

Cindy Harris has worked as a builder at the Centre for Alternative Technology for the last eight years. She was involved in building the self build house there, as well as the Eco-Cabins and the Upper Station for the Cliff Railway, and she teaches on the Centre's self build courses. She is also a member of the advisory panel of the Walter Segal Self Build Trust. A carpenter by training (after a sociology degree) she spends her spare time pulling apart and rebuilding whatever house she happens to be living in. She also enjoys walking and sailing.

Pat and Cindy have also written *The Whole House Book*. See the Resource Guide for details.

Benedicte Foo, an architect, designed the Segal Method Maldwyn Nursery and Family Centre in mid-Wales which was commended in the 1994 Community Enterprise Awards. She was a contributor to the book *Making Space - Women in a Man-Made Environment*, previously taught design on architecture courses, was involved in teaching on Access to Architecture courses and particularly enjoys working with community groups and students.

David Bellamy is a well-known campaigning environmentalist, botanist, author and television presenter, and a patron of the Centre for Alternative Technology.

Brian Richardson, a friend of the late Walter Segal, is an original trustee of the Walter Segal Self Build Trust. As an architect he worked with Segal and Jon Broome on the pioneering Lewisham scheme, and now promotes the method. He is co-author with Jon Broome of *The Self-Build Book*.

Photographic credits: Those not by the authors, or from the libraries of The Centre for Alternative Technology or The Walter Segal Self Build Trust, have been generously lent by: Architype Ltd. (who also provided some drawings), Brian Richardson, David Lea, Excel Industries (Warmcel), Ian McKinnel, Tony Maufe, Rob Ayres (for the photos of trees and bark textures), Mike Daligan's **cover photograph** of the Diggers Self Build Group, Golf Drive, Hollingdean, Brighton, Pat Borer's photo **opposite** of a self build house in Bristol, and Mike Trevillion's photo of the Herefordshire studio interior.

Out of the Woods by Pat Borer and Cindy Harris

© August 1994 and August 1997, The Centre for Alternative Technology and the Walter Segal Self Build Trust. All rights reserved.

The Centre for Alternative Technology
Machynlleth, Powys SY20 9AZ.
Tel. 01654 702400 **Fax**. 01654 702782.
Email: info@cat.org.uk
Website: www.cat.org.uk
Charity No. 265239.

The Walter Segal Self Build Trust
15 High Street, Belford, Northumberland NE70 7NG
Tel. 01668 213544 Fax. 01668 219247.
Website: www.segalselfbuild.co.uk
Charity No. 328130

Advisory panel: Mike Daligan, Brian Richardson.

With assistance from Architype, Lesley Bradnam, Jon Broome, Rick Dance, Benedicte Foo, Peter Harper, Annie Morris, Graham Preston, Vicky Reed.

Illustrations hand coloured by John Urry.

Designed and edited by Dave Thorpe.

Printed on post-consumer waste by Cambrian Printers (01970 627111).

First printing October 1994. **Second edition** July 1997.
Third edition June 2001 **ISBN** 1 898049 12 2.

Published with support, gratefully acknowledged, from the Department of the Environment, Environment Wales and The Tudor Trust.

THANKS
Firstly, our thanks must go to Brian Richardson. He not only co-wrote with Jon Broome the seminal book on the joys of self build called, unsurprisingly, *The Self-Build Book*; but has also given us enthusiastic encouragement, brilliant ideas and withering criticism in appropriate portions whenever asked; and has given us a thoughtful Afterword.

Jon Broome and Jonathan Hines and others of the architectural co-operative Architype have been instrumental in developing the Segal Method in practical, ecologically-sound ways. They have been generous in explaining building constructions and allowing us to raid their picture library for illustrations. Jon Broome wrote the *AJ Special Issue: The Segal Method* booklet which this book attempts to update, and has been most helpful with suggestions for improvements. We should also like to thank David Bellamy for his help in understanding the ecology of timber production and for his Foreword, and Nigel Dudley for the piece on timber certification. Special thanks also to Rob Gwillim for his help with the section on Services; and Peter Harper for his learned support and perceptive comments.

OUT of the WOODS

Environmental Timber Frame Design for Self Build

PAT BORER and CINDY HARRIS

Illustrations by Benedicte Foo and Pat Borer

WALTER SEGAL ■ Self Build Trust

CENTRE FOR
ALTERNATIVE
TECHNOLOGY
PUBLICATIONS

Contents

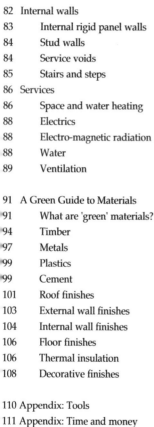

Preface
by David Bellamy

MACHYNLLETH HAS over the past twenty years become a household name for all that is good in alternative technology.

It doesn't matter how it is pronounced - it means wind, water and solar power, biogas, wholefoods, permaculture, recycling, energy conservation, renewable resources, biodegradability. If it's green, it has already flowered and born fruit in the world's most famous recycled slate quarry.

Out of the Woods is its latest publication, jointly with the Walter Segal Self Build Trust. A do-it-yourself *vade mecum* of how to turn your dreams of your house from plans into reality.

A home of your own, built out of nature's own renewable resource - wood. A relatively cheap, easy to work habitat for you, your family and all their possessions, and your own personal share of carbon locked away safely out of the earth's greenhouse.

What is more, built and insulated the Segal way, it is easy to keep warm in winter and cool in summer with minimal use of fossil fuel. Cutting back on acid rain, greenhouse gas emissions and your fuel bill, it is the environmental bargain of the twenty first century. It is relatively earthquake proof and no more of a fire hazard than a conventional home.

Read all about it and then build the home of your dreams. It can even be removed at the end of its life, leaving hardly any trace - the concrete pads on which it rests can be easily removed.

What will Machynlleth dream up next? A grow your own home? Well, if you build yours on a large enough plot and plant the right trees, you'll be able to hand the plans and the resource on to your children.

The only dirty word is "TIMBER!" - except when it's grown sustainably.

Introduction

T HIS BOOK is written for all those of you who may have thought or dreamed of designing and building your own home - or any purpose-built structure. Whether this is a distant dream or on the verge of realisation, we hope to provide inspiration and a practical grounding for your progress.

Too difficult? Not, we suggest, when you decide to work in wood as your principal material. For we are enthusiastic about building in timber. For many people this may seem eccentric at first. Perhaps, recalling the children's tale of the three little pigs and the big, bad wolf, wood appears vulnerable and temporary compared with brick and stone. For reasons that will become clear, this isn't so. For modest buildings - and with a little ingenuity some quite immodest ones - there is no better material for framing, in terms of economy, performance, friendliness, permanence, beauty and ecology, than timber.

We aren't concerned here with the various 'kit' buildings that are currently available. The building method we advocate is far more flexible, adaptable and individually determined. It leads to buildings as unique as the people who design, build and occupy them. That method is called the Segal Method, after the architect who developed it. It uses a particular kind of structural design called post-and-beam timber frame.

What we do is to take you from your ideas to the plans and from your plans to the reality. We look one by one at the many options involved in post and beam design, to help you arrive at the best decisions for your own needs.

We believe that every material you use is important. They may enhance or worsen your living conditions; and their manufacture or disposal may create pollution. We examine them, and your use of fuel and energy, in terms of suitability, economics and environmental impact. In an appendix you can find descriptions of the tools you might use when building. In the resource guide you can discover where to find more information, help, and how to locate many of the materials we discuss.

Faced with a project as ambitious and daunting as building a house, the Segal Method and environmental design can take you out of the woods and put everything in perspective. Furthermore, we believe that self build, being affordable and democratic, offers a path away from the current shortage of housing stock. It is relatively easy for people with no previous building experience to embark on such a project - as plenty already have. Given the will, anyone can do it. Of course, you need two other ingredients - time and money. Rough guidelines as to how much of each can be found on page 111. To some extent these variables are interchangeable. Having a lot of one might mean you need less of the other. For instance, having time to learn and practice a trade before starting work might mean you avoid having to employ a professional Similarly, having time to shop around for lower prices, special offers or used materials (e.g. timber, doors, sanitary fittings, slates and tiles) will reduce costs Conversely, a shortage of time need not slow down the building process if more labour can be bought in or specialist sub-contractors employed.

Britain is known as a nation of D-I-Y-ers. From putting up a shelf, through to a loft conversion or extension, people everywhere are always busy customising their own homes. Self build is the logical extension of that practice and provides the maximum freedom and satisfaction. Many self builders have gained confidence and experience from tackling smaller jobs first. Knowing their strengths and weaknesses, they can decide where best to put their efforts. This could be in the co-ordination and management of a project or a complete involvement with the building work. For most, the experience will lie somewhere in between.

Within your particular financial constraints, it is up to you to decide at every stage who should do what. Starting with the financing of the project, through to the siting, design, layout, materials, building processes and overall management, you can bring in the appropriate professionals - or not. This is the beauty of self build - choice over a whole range of options and different levels of involvement.

Often, individuals group together to form legal entities called housing co-operatives in order to build. The Walter Segal Self Build Trust exists to help you find out how to organise yourselves to do this. Whether you work on your own or in a group, self building makes the best use of your existing skills and gives the opportunity to develop new ones. Your standards of construction work will tend to be very high, because for you it's not just a job - it's something you will have to live with. Ease of maintenance can be built in. Housing can become a process of creation that may continue at any time, even after you have moved in.

There is a particular satisfaction in living in a house that you have physically put together to be just the way you want it. And whatever else, the experience is always remembered as special, as a time of extraordinary intensity, concentration and commitment. It consumed all available time, energy and attention At times it was pure hard slog. But it was also a thrilling adventure...

The housing crisis

IT IS EVERYBODY'S right to have a decent roof over their heads. Yet the scale and severity of Britain's housing crisis has reached catastrophic proportions. The lack of a space to call one's own and the stigma of having 'no fixed address' carry severe social and psychological consequences. The link between bad housing and poor health, particularly for children and the elderly, is now widely recognised. Meanwhile, the housing shortage is such that even those with homes are often trapped in inadequate or sub-standard housing. It has been estimated that houses built today would have to last 4,000 years at the current rate of replacement. Following a recent survey, the National Home Improvement Council reports a 20% deterioration in the U.K. housing stock since 1986, when the estimated national bill for all renovations and repairs stood at £24bn.

There are wider issues too. Efforts to provide decent standards of comfort warmth and economic running costs also contribute towards energy conservation and minimal pollution. We can and should do better than the minimum standards set by the current Building Regulations on insulation levels, which are barely adequate and easily evaded. As well as the dearth of investment in public housing and the lack of incentives to stimulate more private housing, we are suffering the effects of the disastrous policies of the '60s and '70s - high rise system building and mass housing. Gone were the tried and tested craft practices which could be adjusted to accommodate defects, in favour of the 'technical fix', universally applied. Unfortunately, policy makers do not seem to have learned many lessons from these mistakes. In the area of 'social' housing, now increasingly the responsibility of the Housing Corporation, the latest rulings mean there will be fewer, larger Housing Associations, running massive contracts in conjunction with major developers, putting up 'affordable' houses on greenfield sites. The message is the same as in the '60s - standardised, lowest-possible-cost 'units' of accommodation.

In contrast to all of this, the advantages of self build remain relatively unexplored. The opposite of a centralised 'top-down' approach, it relies on people's own enthusiasm and effort. It can provide an element of training and gives people a chance to determine the shape of their surroundings. Its concentration on smaller projects spreads the investment load and avoids huge estates of identical housing, with the social problems they can create.

Until recent times, building your home was the normal thing to do. For most people it was the only way to get a roof over their heads. Landless peasants would complete the shell of a small house in 24 hours, for a right of tenure would be gained if smoke was seen rising from the chimney before sunrise the next day. The first Building Societies were in fact mutual savings clubs, that were dissolved after all their members had built their own homes. In many other parts of the world today, self build is still the most widely used option. In the U.S.A. self-help housing accounts for one in five of all new dwellings, and in some Western European countries, such as France, Belgium, Germany, Italy and Austria, the figure was over half for the 1980s. Britain is one of the few which stands out as failing to promote self build as an option. The experience of those who work in the field is that there is a huge demand which is not being satisfied.

Not everyone would choose to build for themselves, but for those who do it should be a viable option. Access to land and finance could be improved and planning regulations made less restrictive. Deprived of its mystique, the process of building could become much more open, enlarging and enriching the pattern of housing provision in this country.

Ways of building

NATURE, AND HUMANKIND, have found three ways of building: with no firm structure (amoeba, jellyfish, slugs - and inflatables); with an external structure (crabs, insects - and brick, block, earth and cast concrete buildings); and with an internal structure (mammals, birds, nests - and timber, steel or concrete framed buildings).

Below: Structural systems in nature and in building.

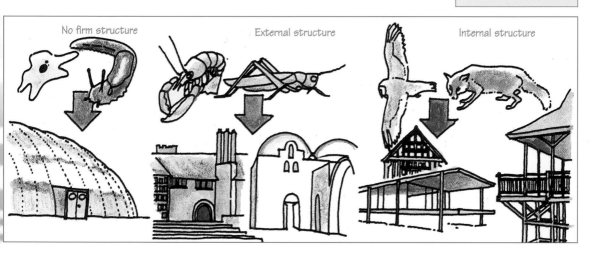

| No firm structure | External structure | Internal structure |

Everywhere in the world where trees are plentiful, timber construction predominates. If there is an abundance, timber can be piled up like masonry to form the walls of the familiar log cabin. Or it can be used structurally as a frame, to be clad. Both traditions survive in heavily timbered countries, but framing has evolved in modern times into two families. As good quality timber became scarce in America, so posts became more slender and were placed closer together to support the shallower beams; machine-made nails became available to join these small pieces, and the timber 'stud' frame was born. Most timber building is now stud framing, with roofs losing their beams and rafters to be covered in light, nailed trusses. Stud framing is an economical way to build, and is the most common form of house construction in North America and Scandinavia, and is becoming so in Scotland.

We believe that timber framing with a post and beam structure is a more suitable building technique for self build than stud framing. We find it exciting to create a completely clear structure of roof, floor and posts into which walls can be placed at will.

Post and Beam Frames

The structural principle of 'post and beam' framing is that loads are carried by small timbers - tiling, lath and studs - which in turn are carried by slightly larger pieces - rafters, floor joists, ceiling joists - to beams, which are supported at larger intervals by posts, which are carried by the founda-tions.

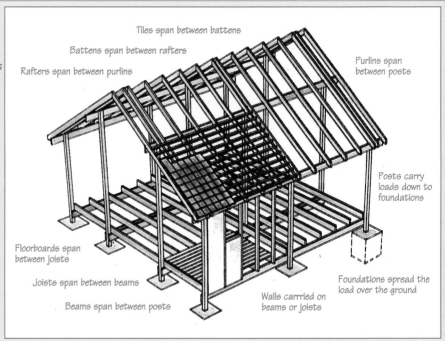

Tiles span between battens

Battens span between rafters

Rafters span between purlins

Purlins span between posts

Posts carry loads down to foundations

Floorboards span between joists

Joists span between beams

Beams span between posts

Walls carrried on beams or joists

Foundations spread the load over the ground

ADVANTAGES
- Planning freedom. As walls are not loadbearing, they can be placed to form the rooms you want;
- Windows and doors can be placed anywhere;
- Few foundations are necessary, as the posts carry all loads to only a few points;
- The roof can be constructed early to provide a sheltered building site;
- Good fire resistance is provided to structural elements;
- The structure can be decorative;
- It is easy to alter the building later;
- Damp is defeated. The building touches the ground in just a few places, where it is sealed.

DISADVANTAGES
- Some high quality, large section, expensive timber is needed;
- The jointing of timber is critical and involves care;
- Infill walls are often strong enough to hold the building up, so posts may be redundant;
- Frames are often heavy to raise;
- Care is needed to keep the structural elements clean, if they are to be exposed to view and decorative.

The Legacy of Walter Segal

THE DEVELOPMENT of post and beam timber frame building owes a great deal to the architect Walter Segal. He refined the building process to its bare bones, in order to make it accessible to all. Among the aspects of his work explored by others after his death are those concerned with its ecological implications, and these particularly interest us.

The idea of giving control over housing to the people who have to live with the results was as revolutionary in the 1970s as it is now. At this time Walter Segal branched away from the conventional career track of an architect, to seek more control over the whole building process.Starting with a

Above: Walter Segal's temporary house in Highgate (1963).

Far left: The first self build house in Woodbridge, Suffolk (1971).

Left: The first self build scheme in Lewisham (1980).

Above: *Self builders in Lewisham.*

Right: *The first self build scheme in Lewisham (1980).*

Far Right: *The second self build scheme in Lewisham (1986).*

Below: *The interior of John Broome's Lewisham self build home.*

temporary house built in his back garden in 1963, Segal developed a highly simplified but technically sophisticated method of building, based on the mediaeval post and beam frame. Aiming to satisfy the demands of speed and economy, he used materials which could be bought off the shelf and assembled on site, with a minimum of cutting and fitting. The design itself was accommodated to the materials available.

Segal also took on those aspects of building traditionally delegated by archi-tects to other professionals. Assuming the roles of structural engineer, quantity surveyor and site supervisor, he ran his own contracts from start to finish. He valued greatly the direct contact he had with his clients, particularly at the design stage. Everything would be decided face-to-face at site meetings. He even denied himself the safety net of professional indemnity insurance. In such ways Segal sought autonomy for himself and others.

This approach led to him being appointed architect for two schemes in Lewisham in the late '70s and early '80s. The Local Authority provided land and finance for tenants on its waiting list to build their own homes. Unlike tradi-tional self build schemes, the Lewisham groups were 'open access'. No formal training or experience were needed, and the groups included a man in his 60s and a single mother, both inexperienced in building.

Segal consulted closely with the self builders at the design stage. Each house, though part of a Council scheme, had its own individual stamp. The plans and drawings originating from these discussions were used, together with other documents, to explain the whole process. A Schedule of Materials (see page 31) itemised each building component, its size, finish and place in the building. This also served as a 'shopping list' from which to obtain competitive quotes. Segal produced a set of building instructions - a step-by-step sequence of operations. The process was made 'transparent' - easily understood and esily controlled.

For several years before he died in 1985, Segal had been coming to the Centre for Alternative Technology to run courses on self build. There was an unspoken

Left: The low-energy self build demonstration house at the Glasgow Garden Festival (1988).

Top Right: Low-energy self build house at the Centre for Alternative Technology, Machynlleth (1987).

Above: Calthorpe Community Centre in King's Cross, London (1991).

but natural affinity between his ideas and those of the Centre, based on a desire to enable and empower people. In the era when environmentalists had concluded that 'small is beautiful', Segal had also chosen to work on small-scale projects. His buildings are modest and unassertive and the process of building them was essentially accessible and democratic. They are appropriate in a way that mass housing can never be.

The low-tech, low-waste approach blended well with the Centre's own ideas, stemming from concerns with environmental conservation.

The self build courses at C.A.T. continue, ably led by Segal's friends and colleagues. The Walter Segal Self Build Trust was formed to promote his ideas and provide assistance to self builders. Followers began to adapt his method to create low-energy houses, like the one built at C.A.T. in 1988.

However, despite this evolution, the central philosophy of his method has remained respected. As Graham Vickers wrote in the *Architects Journal*'s tribute to Segal in 1988, 'The Segal legacy, by its nature, may be seen less as a tangible bequest, more as a trust fund of possibilities.'

Top: *The Hop Farm Visitor Centre, Kent (1991).*

Above: *The Maldwyn Family Centre in Newtown, Powys (1992).*

Ecological timber frame design

THERE ARE SEVERAL good reasons for choosing timber. It is an easy material to work on. The necessary tools are cheap, portable and widely available. Basic woodworking skills are easier to aquire than those required for other structural materials, e.g. steel or masonry. Wood is relatively easy to lift and handle. It also has an immediate aesthetic appeal for many people, making it pleasant to work with. It looks and feels warm and inviting to the touch.

Then there are its structural qualities. It has a good strength-to-weight ratio and performs well under extreme conditions, including hurricanes and earthquakes. Timber can be bought in different structural grades, depending on the load it is expected to carry. The better grades have fewer knots and a straighter grain.

Due to the lack of a continuous tradition of timber building in this country, many people feel that a good quality, solid house has to be made of bricks and mortar. In fact, timber frame buildings can last indefinitely, when properly cared for (see below). They perform well in the event of fire, retaining their structural integrity for a relatively long time. And, properly designed, they have withstood hurricane force winds with virtually no damage (see page 27).

These relatively lightweight timber buildings have the advantage of a quick response to changes in temperature, so will heat up fast when a fire is lit or the heating system is switched on. Unlike high thermal mass buildings, usually made of brick, block or stone, they do not store heat in the building fabric and so will cool down quickly once the heat is turned off.

There are also the environmental advantages of using timber as the main structural component of a building. It is (potentially) a renewable material, and has a low 'embodied energy content' (this refers to all the energy that goes into producing and transporting a product). In the case of timber, it is the sun's energy that produces it, so its embodied energy costs are all in the extraction and transportation of the logs from the forest. If the timber used is locally grown, the energy costs are reduced to the minimum possible.

Most home grown timber is used for low grade products such as fence posts, firewood and chipboard. By specifying such timber for structural use, value is added to it, thereby stimulating re-planting and proper management of British woodlands. Small sections of short length timber, available almost anywhere, can be used for secondary members such as joists and studs.

Timber also acts as a 'sink' for carbon dioxide. Unless it is burned or allowed to rot down, timber will 'lock up' carbon in the cellulose, rather than releasing it as CO_2, adding to the greenhouse effect.

Since we at C.A.T. choose durable species, and detail the building to allow for adequate ventilation, we find it mostly unnecessary to use toxic timber treatments and preservatives (see the Green Guide to Materials).

Is a timber frame house more likely to burn down?

In a severe fire, larger section timbers will char on the outer surface. This charring actually delays the spread of flame and protects the core of the timber. Unlike steel members which, when heated, will suddenly buckle and collapse, timber burns slowly and steadily at a predictable rate. Posts, beams, joists and rafters can therefore be sized to allow time for evacuation. In Sweden, where many houses are of timber, fire insurance is cheaper than for brick houses.

Will a timber frame building last?

There is no reason why not, if properly looked after.

The oldest wooden structures existing today are the Buddhist Golden Hall and Pagoda in Japan, built in the 7th century A.D.

In this country, the oldest example of a timber frame building is an eleventh century stave church in Greenstead, Essex (pictured right). There are also many fine market towns built of timber dating from the fifteenth century, e.g. Shrewsbury and Ludlow. Of all the buildings which have survived from pre-Reformation times, 90% are timber frame.

Left: *London Wildlife Trust garden centre (1991).*

Above: *Pilot self build house for Bristol City Council (1993).*

Minimising impact

PARADOXICALLY, the construction of buildings is also destructive - in terms of the landscape and the production and supply of materials.

Traditionally, buildings were made with locally available, naturally occurring materials such as mud, stone, turf and wood. But the alleged technical superiority and easy availability of modern materials has distanced us from the beneficial effects of using traditional ones. Environmentally sensitive building is about trying to minimise the destructive aspects of current practices.

With the Segal Method of timber framing, much less foundation work is necessary than for conventional buildings, thereby minimising the disruption of the landscape and the use of cement. The building is lifted clear of the ground, which eliminates the dangers associated with the build-up of radon gas. Post and beam frames sit easily on steeply sloping or rocky sites. This opens up the possibility of cheaper plots, as well as helping to limit the encroachment of buildings on to greenfield sites.

The fact that the walls are non-loadbearing means that they can be made of any lightweight material. This increases the design possibilities. For instance, it is easy to make glass the infill material, to take advantage of passive solar gain, without any additional frames being necessary.

The fact that Segal style buildings are not usually fixed to the ground enables them to 'sit lightly upon the earth'. At the end of their life when they are demolished, all that remains are a few concrete pads and service connections, which can be disposed of much more easily than normal foundations, leaving hardly a trace that there ever was a building there.

Energy in buildings

BUILDINGS, in their construction and servicing, account for two thirds of the nation's energy consumption. From an individual perspective, it makes sense to design and build houses that will be cheap to run. On a global level, reducing energy consumption can have a significant impact on reducing global warming and acid rain. We can save energy by conservation measures, such as insulation

Above: Sea Saw self build, Brighton (1994).

and using heat gain from the sun.

The main way of saving energy is to reduce heat loss through the fabric of the building. Timber walls are easier to insulate to a high standard than brick or blockwork walls. Roofs can be designed to allow for the extra depth of insulation (300mm plus) recommended for 'superinsulation' (see page 107). Double or triple glazing will reduce heat loss through windows.

The principles of 'passive solar' can be used in the design, whereby the house itself is designed to collect as much solar energy as possible to help with the heating. The main living room should be on the south side; store rooms, corridors and garages should be placed as 'buffers' on the cold, north side. Large windows should be on the south side, shaded by roof overhangs to reduce overheating by the summer sun. Windows on the north side should be the minimum required for daylighting. Shelter from the north wind (trees, fences, earthworks) could be provided. The main external door should be protected by

Energy ratings for houses

The Government's Standard Assessment Procedure (SAP) produces an energy rating for a dwelling, based on calculated energy costs for space and water heating.

The rating is expressed on a scale of one to a hundred; the higher the number, the better the standard, Other energy ratings - for example NHER and Starpoint - can be converted to an SAP rating and will be referred to in future Building Regulations.

A house built to today's Building Regulations would achieve an SAP of 70. Many Housing Associations require a rating of 75. Segal Method self build houses of the current generation have an SAP rating of 92 to 98.

Some schemes on the drawing board have ratings of over 100. In practice this means the self builders will have lower fuel bills than almost anyone in the country.

an enclosed porch, acting as a buffer and as a solar collector. Timber houses will not be as effective at storing passive solar heat as will 'heavyweight' masonry houses, but it is still worthwhile - the result will be a dwelling that feels light and comfortable.

The self builder can also install a solar water heating system whch contributes significantly to water heating requirements (for details of how to do this, see C.A.T. booklet *Tapping the Sun,* in the Resource Guide).

Self builders as a whole make up a significant and growing share of the market, and, unlike professional builders who must work to standard specifications, are in a position to make environmentally positive choices in design and materials. Who better to do this than those who will reap the benefit of warmth and comfort at low cost?

Designing for self build

ESIGNING A BUILDING is a bit like juggling. Elements such as space, shelter, position, economy, buildability, ecology and a sense of delight all seek a balanced position in your scheme of things; and they all affect each other. You, the designer, are the sole judge of how satisfying the resolution is. For every built design there are a thousand unbuilt solutions that might have been equally satisfactory. The final decision rests on personal choice and inspiration.. But the more information you have about all the variables, the better will be your decision.

You will bring to the decision-making process your experience of other buildings, other features, other spaces and shapes, your idea of beauty, colour preferences and lifestyle demands. These will come face to face with:

- your response to the site;
- your budget;
- heating, lighting and acoustic comfort;
- local planning requirements;
- Building Regulations;
- Health and Safety requirements;
- the environmental effects of your choices and activities;
- the way the building may affect your health and mood;
- its buildability;
- and, finally, its subsequent ease of maintenance.

Your ideas may be drawn from centuries of vernacular building. These are at their most appropriate from your particular area, since local builders in times past will have faced many of the same problems you face and solved them with local, natural materials. These materials are quite often the most environmentally suitable and the finished building should blend well in the locality.

You can also find inspiration in other parts of the world where the climate, culture and building techniques are familiar.

To focus your ideas, you could do no better than to browse through two books by Christopher Alexander, *The Timeless Way of Building* and *A Pattern Language*. The titles alone indicate that there are ways of organising buildings that may particularly satisfy the human spirit; universal living patterns that transcend local custom.

Slowly, through a circular, iterative process, your plans will emerge. You will bring in different, often conflicting requirements, go back to the beginning, work through the process again, until the design is created. The first image to materialise is probably a floor plan. This is the basic, generally understood, graphic representation of a building. Small children can interpret such a plan as a miniature, bird's eye view of the world.

The tartan grid

Walter Segal used a 'tartan' grid. The narrow areas represent the wall and structure zone and are the same thickness as the walling panel, joist, beam and timber post used (50mm). As there is a 50mm gap between wall panels, they can be arranged in any configuration without cutting. The larger grid zone is 600mm - a common width of sheet materials. Posts are 50mm wide to fit within the tartan, but as their depth is greater (say 175mm), they project partly outside the grid and walls. Ceiling panels 600mm wide will fit between 50mm wide joists without cutting.

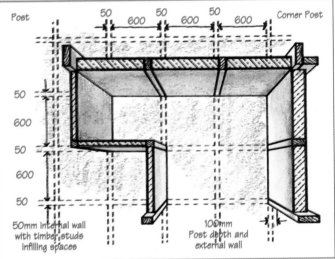

ADVANTAGES
- Wall and ceiling panels can be loose-fit and re-usable;
- Materials cutting is minimised;
- The gaps between panels can be used for services.

DISADVANTAGES
- Column width is limited to smaller tartan dimension;
- Gaps between panels can lead to poor thermal and acoustic performance;
- Quite a lot of material is required to cover gaps.

The plan indicates the proximity, purposes and relative sizes of different rooms. Its orientation and position is your response to the site. Its walls are determined by the kind of structure you require; if you want to live in a greenhouse, a light skeletal structure is required. If living underground is your ambition, you'll need massive masonry walls.

Walter Segal's approach gives the designer as wide and flexible a choice as possible, within a particular framework. This is a simple, clear construction method, where freedom of planning is combined with economy. The Segal Method is not an industrialised building system with special manufactured components. It is a way of building that uses ordinary building materials and simple construction techniques to give substance to your design.

The essential Segal Method

THE ELEMENTS common to all the constructional patterns we explore are:
- A post and beam frame giving strength, clarity, flexibility and openness;
- A simple building process and easily understood techniques;
- Non-loadbearing walls set out on a grid to keep waste to a minimum;
- Readily available materials in their market sizes and finishes;
- Foundations and groundworks kept to a minimum;
- Materials selected for each application according to the criteria of performance, cost, ecological considerations and beauty;
- Logical and thorough documentation.

Most self builders will require some professional help to guide them through the planning and building processes - a person who can point out the financial, structural, aesthetic or regulatory implications of design decisions; sketching alternatives and suggesting constructional choices.

The centreline grid

The most common grid used in conventional timber stud frame construction can be used for post and beam. Structural members are completely covered by sheet materials.

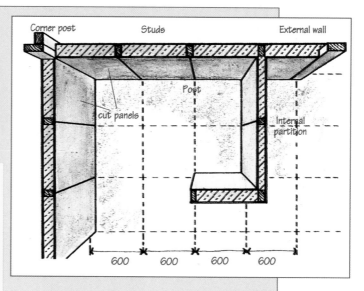

ADVANTAGES
• Wall and ceiling panels can be fixed direct to studs/joists;
• Loose-fill insulation can be used;
• Sheet materials can be used structurally.

DISADVANTAGES
• Materials have to be cut on corners and junctions of external and internal walls;
• Windows and doors adjacent to posts have to be a non-modular size;
• There is no 'services void' between wall panels;
• The structure is not visible, which can result in featureless rooms.

The architect (or other experienced helper) must have a thorough knowledge of the structural principles of timber design, and be able to prove the structure by calculation. They must also be able to schedule all the building materials needed; advise on site programming; explain every detail and construction process to a lay builder; and assess energy and ecological implications. Walter Segal was convinced that the best designs will come via an architect who is thoroughly at home with all the technical matters involved in a house, and who is in close personal touch with the builder.

Working with the Segal Method

THE FIRST STEP in making a plan is to use a grid. The dimensions of the grid's unit squares match those of commonly available building materials, therefore minimising the amount of cutting to fit. Your plan sits on this grid and superimposed on the grid lines are the doors, windows and walls. The dimensions of these are multiples of the unit lengths. You can therefore use squared paper to design the layout.

Vertical dimensions are similarly determined by the dimensions of the materials used.

It follows that post and beam frames relate to the grid lines. There are two main grid types, called 'tartan' and 'centreline'. The diagrams display the chief features of each. Each grid depends mainly on the type of construction to be used, but also on aesthetic, ecological and planning preferences. Neither one is perfect; both have advantages and disadvantages, as you can see from the boxes.

The two grid types can be combined and adapted to suit individual constructions. The wall/structure zone of a tartan grid can be made irregular to accommodate thicker, better insulated walls and stouter posts which will support more weight. For example the 'Low Energy Self Build House' at C.A.T. has 100mm

The choice of grid dimensions

The two main choices for the panel width are illustrated, together with their advantages and disadvantages.

600mm panel width

ADVANTAGES
• Wide choice of materials is available;
• Common materials are designed to span this distance.

DISADVANTAGES
• Planning is sometimes awkward.

450/900mm panel width

ADVANTAGES
• Planning can be more convenient.

DISADVANTAGES
• There is a limited choice of materials;
• 450mm is often uneconomic, 900mm is too large for common materials to span and units are heavy to handle.

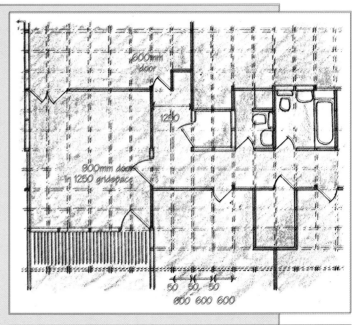

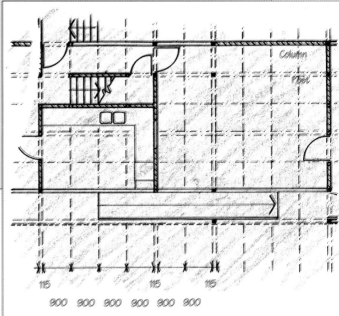

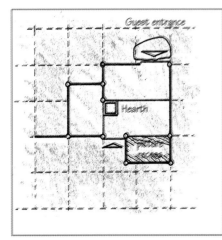

Left: Japanese room sizes were based on floor mat (tatami) dimensions.
This is a floor plan of a standard tea-room with $2^{3}/_{4}$ mats, $^{1}/_{2}$ ken grid (1 ken - 650mm).
From: H. Engel: The Japanese House, a Tradition for Contemporary Architecture.

hick walls and 100mm square posts, which occur every four grid units or nodules. Construction of highly insulated external walls can sometimes be simplified by using a conventional centreline grid. As sheet materials now meet at the gridlines (centrelines) they can be nailed to timber verticals (studs) to provide a stiff wall and contain loose fill insulation.

Walter Segal used a panel width of 600mm, as the common sheet materials are made in increments of this width. His structural zone was 50mm wide, since the woodwool panels he used are 50mm thick and timber is available in the same thickness. But other dimensions are possible. Panel widths may be 900mm (corridor or door width), 450mm or 400mm, to suit the materials chosen or particular planning strategies. Structural zones may be 50, 75, 100, 125, 150mm or more, to suit wall thicknesses and post sections.

Making a plan

WHEN DESIGNING a building plan, the self builder will take their sheet of squared paper and make each square represent a grid 'module' (600mm, 900mm, etc.). It is helpful if this sketch plan shows furniture, bathroom and kitchen fittings, to give a sense of scale; and to make sure the layout and circulation work happily. A post and beam structure can then be introduced that will carry the weight of the floors, roof, walls and the imposed 'loads' from people, furniture, wind and snow. As the walls take no weight they can be placed anywhere, as can windows and doors - indeed the walls could be completely glazed. It is possible to re-arrange the wall elements after the building is completed; to add another bedroom, or (it has been done) take down a partition to combine two rooms for a party.

Along with this simplified approach to building goes a common-sense attitude to the building plans - the documentation needed to turn the idea into reality. Walter Segal provided his self builders with appropriate instructions for each task: clear plans; a shopping list of all materials; written instructions and annotated sketches of critical parts.

Below: Beginning the self builders' process of designing their house: initial ideas and the resulting 'bubble' diagram.

"...the thought processes in the planning of our house were as follows...
'We used the C.A.T. designs for ideas for the general sizing of bedrooms and bathroom etc., & then moved onto graph paper - which was great fun and simple to do with the modular layout
"About size, we asked ourselves - how much space do we need? We're happy with the space we have now so will keep room sizes similar to present house. Costs! - what can we afford to build? And heat? And clean?!
"What about layout? Open plan kitchen/living area - gives feeling of space. Central woodburning stove. Compact bathroom - spend least time in there. Composting loo. Main bedroom near bathroom. Sleeping areas apart. Southish facing conservatory for solar gain & view - with access from living area. Entrance porch to 'drip in' & to act as buffer to north face. Storage space - loft a must!"

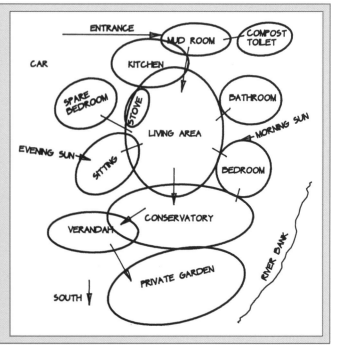

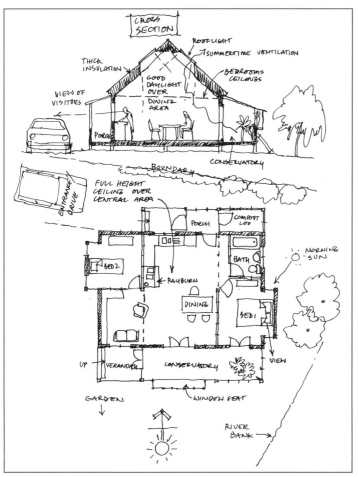

Most of Walter's buildings had flat roofs, which, as the roof shape will just follow the ins and outs of any plan shape, gives the designer complete planning freedom. The wall elements are interchangeable, being all of the same height - usually a standard panel height of 2400mm. A pitched roof, with roof-shaped internal spaces, complicates and imposes a discipline on planning, and wall panels will have to be cut to fit the roof slope. The decision over roof shape will therefore have an influence over planning decisions.

We hope that this book, which sets out to explore building possibilities, demonstrates the range of construction possible within the Segal Method and will inform your choice. There will still be conflicts between various decisions - that is the substance of design. Out of the vast building pattern-book that constitutes Design we are exploring techniques and materials that we feel make for a natural way of construction suitable for self builders - post and beam timber frame.

Sketch plans evolving from the 'bubble diagram' overleaf:

Above: Sketch of house.

Right: Floor plan sketch over graph paper.

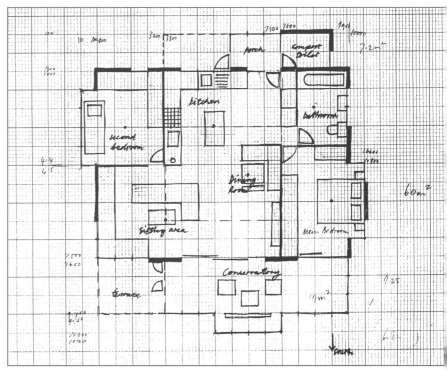

Getting on site

Having decided on the plan and form of the building, a structure will need to be devised. The structural design may well affect earlier decisions - matters of energy conservation, building regulations, site restraints and opportunities, and cost all need to be fed into the equation.

Eventually some formal drawings can be prepared for discussions with Local Authority planners, which will lead to a Planning Application (for which there is a fee). The Planning Application process - consulting with interested bodies - takes about two months and leads up to a decision at the Local Authority Planning Committee Meeting. Meanwhile, if you are confident of the outcome of your Planning Application, work can proceed on preparing drawings and other documents for an application for consent under the Building Regulations (for which there is another fee).

The plans submitted for consent have to show the scheme in sufficient detail to convince the Building Control Officer

Above: *A sketch can help you decide the form and structure you want.*

that the construction will comply with all the Building Regulations, and often with the requirements of the Fire Officer and the Health and Safety Executive.

Of special interest in a Segal Method building will be structural calculations to prove strength and stability - that it will not collapse under everyday loadings or under the weight of snow; and that it can resist forces from high winds.

Formal consent will normally take eight weeks to come through. There will usually be a to-ing and fro-ing of letters to clear up questions - particularly those related to the structure, which may be novel to the engineers engaged in checking the calculations. Building Control Officers are usually helpful people,

Will a timber frame building blow away?

No. You or your architect will check that the construction method and materials specified are sufficient to resist the forces of:

1. Uplift: 2. Overturning: 3. Racking: 4. Sliding

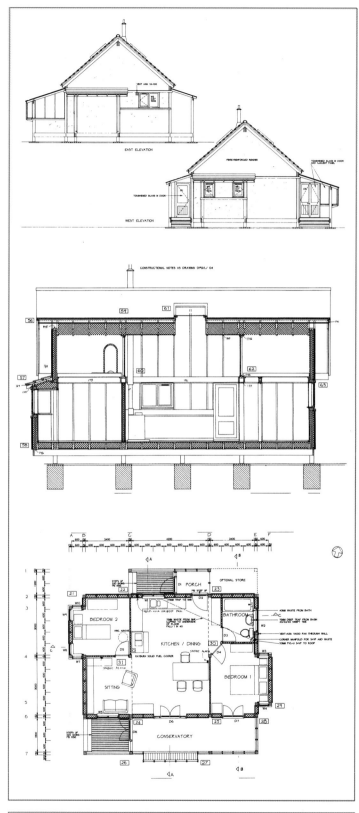

Above: Examples of elevation, cross-section and plan drawings.

whose practical advice is invaluable on site.

The final working drawings can now be prepared, together with a 'shopping list' and specification of all the materials required, and written instructions. The quantity of information needed by the self builder is greater than that normally supplied to a professional builder - as everything has to be explained: perhaps sixty drawings and sketches, and a slim volume of instructions and lists.

The self builder now needs to:

i) Understand how the building is constructed, by checking the shopping list off against the drawings. This checks the accuracy of the list, and helps the self builder construct a mental picture of the building.

ii) Obtain quotations for the materials on the shopping list.

iii) Arrange for services connections (electricity, water, sewage, gas, phone).

iv) Arrange site insurance, buy or hire tools, create a secure store, etc.

Eventually the day will dawn when work on site can begin. Successful building is all about planning ahead and doing work in the correct sequence: being ready for delivery and storage of materials; making sure deliveries occur when, not before, they are needed; making enough room for scaffolding or for raising frames; keeping vulnerable materials dry; planning ahead for services; finishing a job before starting on the next; etc. The diagram on page 32 shows the general process of designing and building.

The resources (with their limitations and possibilities) are:
• yourself (and partner(s), friends and hired help);
• your architect;
• the land;
• your finance.

The 'official' hurdles to cross are:
• Planning Permission;
• Building Regulations.

The design proceeds in a circular manner right through the building phase - and even after completion. The construction will proceed in a more or

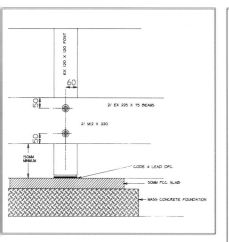

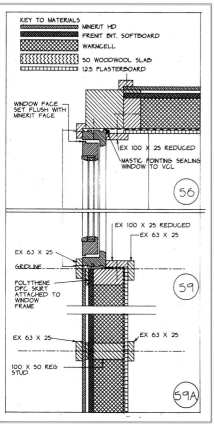

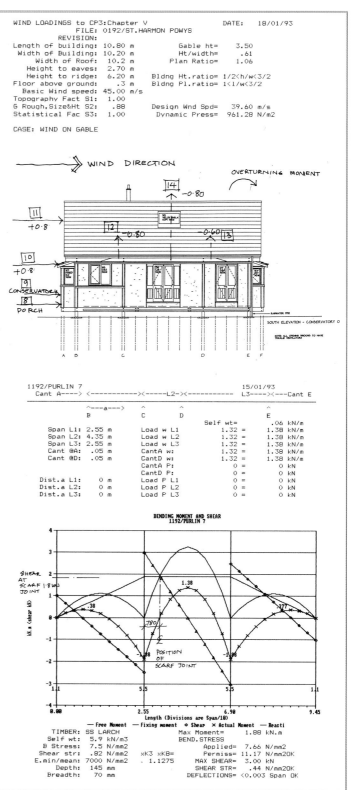

ess logical sequence along a critical path (i.e., some jobs cannot start until others have finished).

This sequence we explore in the next chapter.

Top: *Detail of a framing joint.* **Above:** *Details of wall construction.*
Right: *Examples of structural calculations showing (top) wind loadings and (below) the bending moments in a beam.*

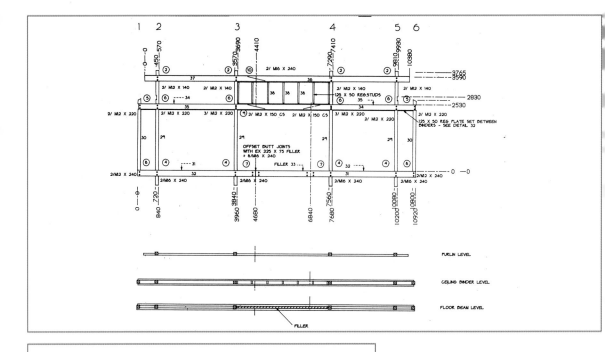

PURLIN LEVEL

CELING BINDER LEVEL

FLOOR BEAM LEVEL

FILLER

Construction Manual   *Sea Saw Self Build*   *Page 13*

Erecting frames

7. *Make sure that everyone remains firmly holding onto the frame until it is securely braced.*

8. Adjust position until square with foundation lines and check frame is vertical with spirit level.

9. Nail pushers to pegs driven into the ground to brace diagonally.

10. Nail horizontal 50 x 75s from bottom of column to the ground pegs to complete temporary brace to 1st frame.

11. *Ensure that the frame is absolutely secure before erecting the next frame.*

Erect further main frames:-

12. Fix pullers and pushers as before.

13. Carefully erect as before - the pullers from each previous frame should rest on top of the next frame ground floor beam as it is erected.

14. Fix spacing battens between frames at ground and first floor levels at the column positions thus ensuring that spacing between frames is correct.

15. Check vertical and diagonals from first frame.

16. Fix pushers and pullers to bottom across between frames forming a cross brace.

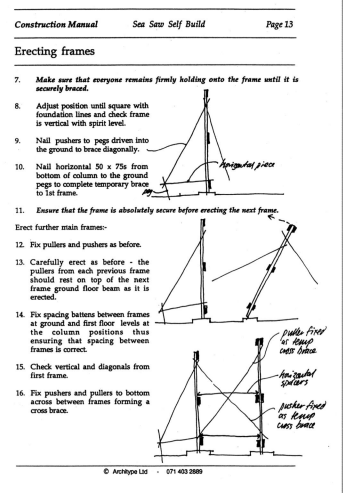

horizontal piece

peg

puller fixed as temp cross brace

horizontal spacers

pusher fixed as temp cross brace

© Architype Ltd   -   071 403 2889

ITEM	GRADE	FINISH	SIZE			UNIT	A	B	C	D	E	F	G	H	I	J	K	L	M	N	O	P	Q	R	S	T	U	V	W	X	TOTAL
CLIENT Chichester Diocesan Housing Associatio	**SITE** Sea Saw Self Build, Vines Cross Road, Brighton									**SCHEDULE**				**STRUCTURAL TIMBER**																
													PLOT LETTER																
FRAMES	*All timber to comply with requirements of accompanying specification*																													
MAIN COLUMNS	SS	sawn	Ex 75	x	175	3600	1	1	1	1	1	1	1	1	1	1	1	1	1	1	1	1	1	1	1	1	1	1	1	1	24
	SS	sawn	Ex 75	x	175	3900	1	1	1	1	1	1	1	1	1	1	1	1	1	1	1	1	1	1	1	1	1	1	1	1	24
	SS	sawn	Ex 75	x	175	4500	1	1	1	1	1	1	1	1	1	1	1	1	1	1	1	1	1	1	1	1	1	1	1	1	24
	SS	sawn	Ex 75	x	175	5400	2	2	2	2	2	2	2	2	2	2	2	2	2	2	2	2	2	2	2	2	2	2	2	2	48
	SS	sawn	Ex 75	x	175	6000	2	2	2	2	2	2	3	2	2	2	2	2	2	2	2	2	2	2	2	2	2	2	2	2	49
	SS	sawn	Ex 75	x	175	6300	2	2	2	2	2	2	3	2	2	2	2	2	2	2	2	2	2	2	2	2	2	2	2	2	49
	SS	sawn	Ex 75	x	175	6900	2	1	2	1	1	2	1	2	2	2	2	2	2	2	2	1	1	2	2	1	1	1	2		39
	SS	sawn	Ex 75	x	175	7200	1	2	1	2	2	1	2	1	1	1	1	1	1	1	1	2	2	1	1	2	2	2	1		33
GROUND & FIRST FLOOR BEAMS	SS	PAR	Ex 75	x	250	6300	4	4	4	4	4	4	4	4	4	4	4	4	4	4	4	4	4	4	4	4	4	4	4	4	96
	SS	PAR	Ex 63	x	250	6300	4	4	4	4	4	4	4	4	4	4	4	4	4	4	4	4	4	4	4	4	4	4	4	4	96
	SS	PAR	Ex 50	x	250	3900						4																			4
	SS	PAR	Ex 50	x	250	4500	1	1	1	1	1	1	1	1	1	1	1	1	1	1	1	1	1	1	1	1	1	1	1	1	24
	SS	PAR	Ex 50	x	250	6300	1	1	1	1	1	1	1	1	1	1	1	1	1	1	1	1	1	1	1	1	1	1	1	1	24
	SS	PAR	Ex 50	x	250	6600	1	1	1	1	1	1	1	1	1	1	1	1	1	1	1	1	1	1	1	1	1	1	1	1	24
	SS	PAR	Ex 50	x	250	6900	1	1	1	1	1	1	1	1	1	1	1	1	1	1	1	1	1	1	1	1	1	1	1	1	24
ROOF BEAMS	SS	PAR	Ex 75	x	225	7200	2	2	2	2	2	2	2	2	2	2	2	2	2	2	2	2	2	2	2	2	2	2	2	2	48
	SS	PAR	Ex 63	x	225	7200	2	2	2	2	2	2	2	2	2	2	2	2	2	2	2	2	2	2	2	2	2	2	2	2	48
22.5 degrees 225mm	SS	PAR	Ex 50	x	225	4500							2																		2

Above: *Example of a 'Schedule of Materials'.*

Right: *At last, building work can get underway.*

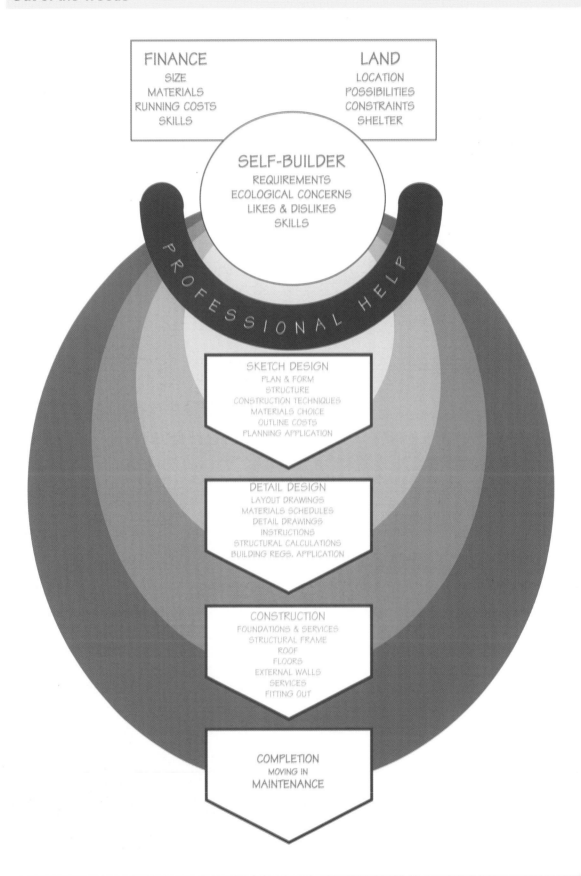

FINANCE
SIZE
MATERIALS
RUNNING COSTS
SKILLS

LAND
LOCATION
POSSIBILITIES
CONSTRAINTS
SHELTER

SELF-BUILDER
REQUIREMENTS
ECOLOGICAL CONCERNS
LIKES & DISLIKES
SKILLS

PROFESSIONAL HELP

SKETCH DESIGN
PLAN & FORM
STRUCTURE
CONSTRUCTION TECHNIQUES
MATERIALS CHOICE
OUTLINE COSTS
PLANNING APPLICATION

DETAIL DESIGN
LAYOUT DRAWINGS
MATERIALS SCHEDULES
DETAIL DRAWINGS
INSTRUCTIONS
STRUCTURAL CALCULATIONS
BUILDING REGS. APPLICATION

CONSTRUCTION
FOUNDATIONS & SERVICES
STRUCTURAL FRAME
ROOF
FLOORS
EXTERNAL WALLS
SERVICES
FITTING OUT

COMPLETION
MOVING IN
MAINTENANCE

Construction: Stages and Choices

T HE ADVANTAGE of the Segal Method of building is its simplicity. It therefore has wide appeal. To help you design your own building, this section looks at each stage of the construction process in turn and identifies the choices available, complete with the advantages and disadvantages of each option. This way you can make a series of informed choices about your design.

Summary of the Segal Method construction stages

Foundations and site works
- Construct the access road, if necessary.
- Install temporary services and site hut.
- Set out and clear the site, strip the topsoil.
- Dig trenches for drains and services.
- Dig foundation pads and fill them with concrete.
- Install drains and services.

Structural frame
- Sort and stack the first timber delivery.
- Mark out, cut, drill and assemble the timber into frames.
- Stack the frames in reverse order of raising.
- Raise the first frame and brace it to the ground.
- Raise the subsequent frames, space them off from each other the correct distance and brace.
- 'Square-up' the frames and put a damp proof course under each post.
- You can now see the building's shape.

External skin: roof
- Install scaffolding around the roof perimeter.
- Cut and fit roof timbers (rafters, joists or purlins).
- Install roof covering (tiles or slates on battens, turf on a membrane on a timber deck, conservatory glazing, or whatever).
- Fix fascias, bargeboards and gutters, soil and vent pipes.
- Re-erect scaffolding to suit constructing the external walls.
- You now have some shelter from the weather.

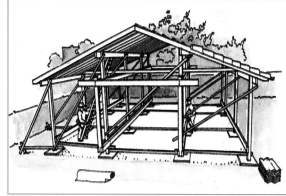

External skin: floor

- Cut and fit the floor joists and insulation supports.
- Fit a temporary floor (floorboards upside down to keep them clean).
- You now have a sheltered workshop. The floor will be completed later, after the building is completely weathertight and services have been installed.

External skin: walls, windows and doors

- Decide on positions of the windows and doors.
- Construct the timber studwork.
- Fit external sheathing, windows and doors.
- Fit external finish (timber weatherboarding, sheeting and coverstrips or render).
- Your building is now weathertight.

Internal walls, services, insulation and finishes

- Install 'first fix' wiring and plumbing.
- Insulate the roof, walls and floor.
- Fix the flooring.
- Construct the internal wall studwork and door frames.
- Decorate and fix the internal wall and ceiling finish (usually plasterboard with timber coverstrips).
- Build stairs, external steps and ramps.
- Finish conservatory, verandah (if any).
- Install 'second fix' electrics and plumbing fittings, heating radiators, bathroom and kitchen fittings.
- Fit internal doors.
- Commission heating, connect electrics to the mains.
- Finish floors.
- Complete landscaping, roads, paths.
- You can now move in.

How to use this chapter

C HOOSING from the construction vocabulary in this chapter is an essentia part of the design process. Some of the following choices have evolve over the last thirty years of Segal Method building. Most have been in us for as long as timber buildings have been around.

No decision can be made in isolation, without reference to the factors outline in earlier chapters. In particular, the post and beam structure itself is so much a integral part of the building that matters such as frame layout and form, span c timbers and post positions, must be worked out as the design progresses, rathe than added later.

Similarly, the type of external enclosure or 'skin' of the building will ofte affect the type of planning grid used which will in turn influence room size structural dimensions and so on.

This chapter is laid out in the order of building, which was summarised o the previous two pages. The topics are 'flagged' at the outside of each page t make it easy to find your way around. You will find a short description of th work at the beginning of each item, usually followed by the differen construction techniques that could be used, with their advantages and disadvar tages listed.

Left: *Siteworks: set out site; strip topsoil; lay drains and services; dig foundation holes, fill with concrete and top with paving slabs.*

The first job on site is to clear away and save topsoil from the 'footprint' of the building and dig holes for foundations, to be filled with concrete. Drainage and services connections are also installed at this stage. The exposed soil under the suspended ground floor needs covering with a damp-proof membrane weighed down with some gravel. To contain this, and give a neat edge, Segal Method buildings often have a row of paving slabs laid round the foundation perimeter. This whole area can now be a relatively clean one in which to construct frames.

A feature of the Segal Method is that the ground floor stands above the ground rather than being laid on it. Foundations are only required under the posts. This minimises messy groundworks and reduces the amount of concrete used to about 20% of that needed for conventional strip foundations.

Sloping sites can be easily accommodated by cutting the posts to suit, the foundation tops following the site contours. The posts rest on the foundation pads, rather than being built in or anchored down - the building's own weight keeps it in position. Once the frames have been raised their positions can be adjusted to make the building square - the need for accurate setting out of foundations is minimised. A damp-proof course is slipped under each timber post to prevent rising damp.

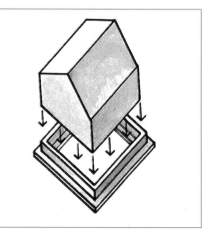

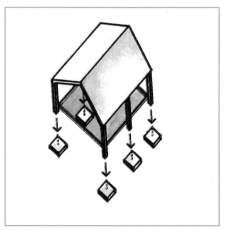

Left: *Two common foundation types: continuous strip (far left) and separate pads.*

foundations: square pads

As each post has its own foundation, the size of these needs only to be sufficient t spread the load safely over the subsoil - usually an area about 600mm square. Th hole will need to be deep enough to avoid frost 'heave' - usually 750 to 900mm Weak soils or made-up ground may require more elaborate foundations. Squar pads can be dug by hand or JCB excavator. A JCB cannot dig a square sided hole, s temporary plywood shuttering will need to be used to save wasting concrete.

ADVANTAGES
- Foundation holes can be hand dug (low cost and accessible for difficult sites);
- Position of holes can be easily adjusted;
- The width of pad allows adjustment of the frames after raising, thus allowing setting-out to be less accurate;
- The relative heights of the pad-tops is not important as the posts are cut to suit.

DISADVANTAGES
- Hand-digging is slow;
- JCB-digging can be wasteful of concrete and damaging to the site.

Right: Foundation pads on a sloping site at Maldwyn Family Centre, Newtown, Powys.

Right: Making a square pad using a JCB; and the finished pad.

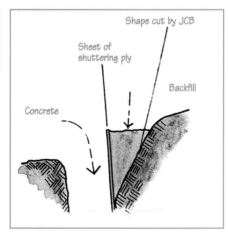

Shape cut by JCB

Sheet of shuttering ply

Backfill

Concrete

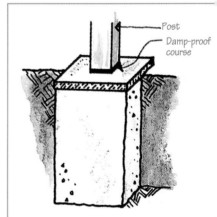

Post

Damp-proof course

Tractor-mounted auger drills are available in various diameters (450, 600, 750mm) that can quickly bore out circular foundation pad holes. The size will depend on the soil's bearing capacity and the loads to be taken - generally 600mm diameter will suffice for domestic buildings.

Whether square or round, the hole is filled with concrete up to ground level, and topped with a paving slab to provide a smooth surface.

ADVANTAGES
- Boring is a fast and neat operation;
- There is little concrete wastage.

DISADVANTAGES
- Hiring machinery is expensive;
- Setting-out has to be more accurate;
- The auger cannot deal with boulder-filled ground;
- Access must be good.

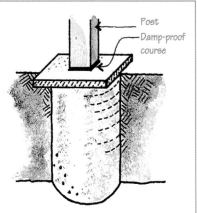

Above: *Boring a foundation hole with a mechanical auger at Jon Broome's house, Lewisham, South London.*

Left: *A round bored pad.*

foundations: piers

Concern is sometimes expressed that the feet of the timber posts are vulnerabl to rot, as they are sitting at ground level. The foundation top can retain wate and earth and leaves may collect around the post. To alleviate this, masonr piers (of brick, block, stone or cast concrete) can be inserted to keep the post bas clear of the ground (see also page 97 regarding treatments).

If these piers are built first, they are very vulnerable to being knocked ove during frame-raising. To overcome this, it seems best to raise the frames a normal on the foundation; jack each post in turn, cut off the excess timber an slide in a pre-cast concrete pier on a bed of mortar.

ADVANTAGES	DISADVANTAGES
• Water can drain away from the post base easily; • Leaves and other debris will not collect around the post base.	• Setting-out has to be very accurate; • Brick-laying skills may be required; • Piers will be more costly than simple pads; • It is an extra operation.

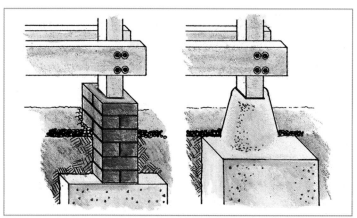

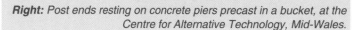

Above Left: Brick or block pier. Right: Concrete pier cast in a bucket.

Right: Post ends resting on concrete piers precast in a bucket, at the Centre for Alternative Technology, Mid-Wales.

Some people find the gap between the building and the ground disturbing - this can be filled with timber boarding or similar. On steep sites where the floor is some way above the ground, the undercroft (space under the ground floor) can provide a useful storage area. If the posts rest on masonry piers, the gap can be filled in by a non-loadbearing masonry wall sitting on a strip foundation. However, the Segal Method's advantage of minimal foundations is then lost.

ADVANTAGES
- The plinth wall helps support the piers during frame-raising;
- The underside of building is less vulnerable to litter accumulation, animals, etc.;
- It is easier to accommodate access ramps, flower beds, etc.

DISADVANTAGES
- It is expensive in materials and time;
- Masonry skills are required;
- Setting-out has to be accurate;
- Foundations are as extensive as for a conventional house.

Above: *The Eco-Cabins at the Centre for Alternative Technology, Mid-Wales were built on a slope. The space underneath has become a wood store and, at this end, provides access to the compost storage vaults in the composting toilet.*

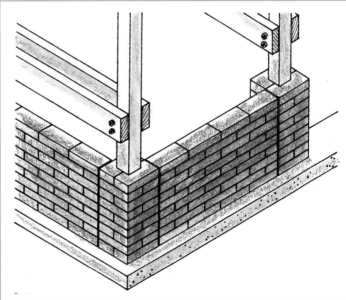

Above: *Strips and plinth wall.*

structural frame

Right: *Making frames: timber is sorted, marked out, cut to length and jointed together.*

The primary structure consists of a series of frames of posts and beams jointed together, assembled flat on the site, raised to vertical and then braced together. Although frames can be raised piecemeal, post by post and beam by beam, raising whole frames is a delightful communal enterprise where, after just a few hours work, the form of the whole building is dramatically revealed.

It is an exhilarating, potentially hazardous business: the mechanics of the process needs careful consideration; the effort required (lifting moment) must be calculated; pushing poles of the correct length should be bolted to the posts; and sufficient, well-briefed people be involved.

The layout of posts and beams is derived from the mixture of planning, structural and aesthetic considerations. The most basic decision is that of roof shape and covering; Walter Segal's original flat roof design allows for the maximum flexibility in planning at the lowest cost, but many prefer the aesthetic and rain-shedding properties of a pitched roof.

Right: *Frame raising: frames are raised and braced rigidly together.*

Left: *Raising a frame by hand at a house in Sheffield (1990).*

Frame raising needs to be well-organised and worked out beforehand if accidents are to be avoided.

If the site is constricted, frames are assembled and stacked in reverse order of raising. The first frame is raised on its foundation pads, brought to vertical and each post securely braced back to the ground with struts. The remaining frames are raised on their pads, spaced apart from each other the correct modular distance, made vertical and braced to the first frame and each other. The temporary braces remain until the building is permanently braced. Once the whole frame structure is square and braced, the secondary timbers (joists, rafters) are fixed at floor and roof level, spaced at the modular grid dimensions.

It is possible (see spreadsheet overleaf) to calculate the 'lifting moment' required - experience shows that about 16 kN.m is the limit to frame-raising by human power. The graph overleaf shows the force that each of the three groups of people will be exerting as the frame is raised.

frame-raising

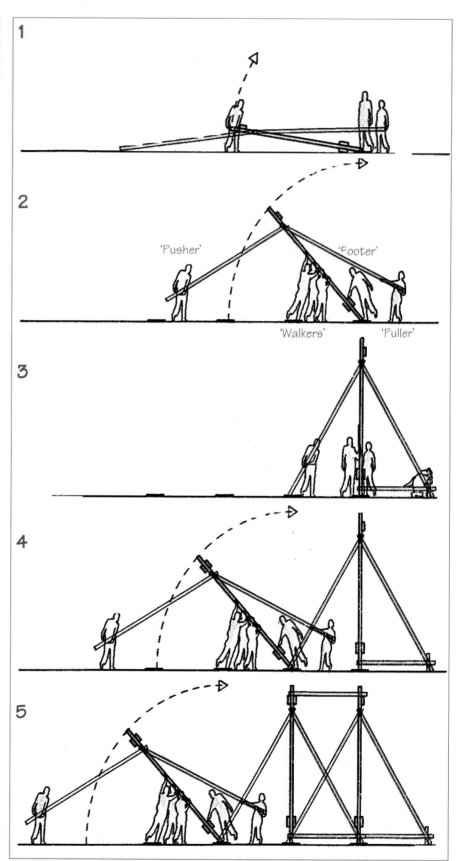

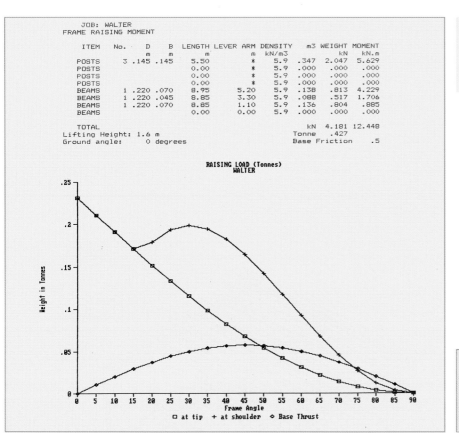

```
JOB: WALTER
FRAME RAISING MOMENT

    ITEM   No.    D     B   LENGTH LEVER ARM DENSITY    m3 WEIGHT MOMENT
                  m     m      m        m     kN/m3           kN     kN.m
    POSTS   3 .145 .145    5.50       *      5.9    .347  2.047  5.629
    POSTS                  0.00       *      5.9    .000   .000   .000
    POSTS                  0.00       *      5.9    .000   .000   .000
    POSTS                  0.00       *      5.9    .000   .000   .000
    BEAMS   1 .220 .070    8.95      5.20    5.9    .138   .813  4.229
    BEAMS   1 .220 .045    8.85      3.30    5.9    .088   .517  1.706
    BEAMS   1 .220 .070    8.85      1.10    5.9    .136   .804   .885
    BEAMS                  0.00      0.00    5.9    .000   .000   .000

    TOTAL                                            kN   4.181 12.448
Lifting Height: 1.6 m                           Tonne    .427
Ground angle:     0 degrees                     Base Friction     .5
```

Left: *Graph showing the relationship between the angle of a frame and the weight bearing down.*

The four stages of frame raising

1. The frame is carried to its position, with the post feet on their foundations. 'Pushing poles' and 'pulling poles' are bolted to the post tops. They must be short enough to provide useful lift as the frame goes up, but long enough to act as temporary bracing to the adjacent frame. They must be free to swing about their bolt.

2. The frame-raisers are distributed thus:
i) One person directing operations and explaining everyone's role.
ii) One person positioned at the base of each post to stop it slipping away
iii) One person per pole, to push, pull and balance the frame as it nears vertical.
iv) Everybody else divided into equal strength teams to lift and 'walk down' each post. The tallest are situated nearest the post top.
   On command, the top of the frame is lifted and raised. At an angle of about 30° the geometry of the process results in the apparent weight increasing for the 'walkers', and decreasing for the 'pushers' and 'pullers' (see the graph above).

3. When the frame is vertical, everybody must remain at their post until the braces are securely fixed. Each post is brought into plumb and properly triangulated back to a stake in the ground.

4. Subsequent frames are raised in the same way. Each is set the correct distance away from the previous frame, and, when plumb, is triangulated back to that frame. Braces must remain until permanent bracing is in place.

frames:
flat roof frame

This option is the cheapest and easiest to build. The roof perimeter simply follows the plan shape, and posts are disposed along the frames to suit structural and planning requirements.

ADVANTAGES
- Provides infinite planning flexibility;
- Post and beam joints are all at right angles;
- A flat roof is easy to lay and safer to work on than a pitched roof;
- All the walls are of the same height.

DISADVANTAGES
- There is a limited choice of finishes for the flat roof;
- Water is not 'shed' off the roof - and any leaks are hard to find.
- No loft space or place for water tanks.

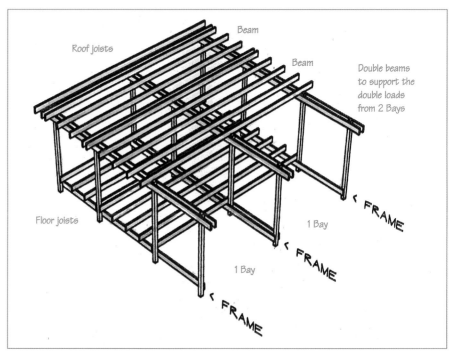

Beam

Roof joists

Beam

Double beams to support the double loads from 2 Bays

Floor joists

< FRAME

1 Bay

< FRAME

1 Bay

< FRAME

Left: *Flat roof frames on the Lewisham self build house (1980).*

A purlin is the name given to a horizontal beam that supports sloping secondary members (rafters). Purlin frames run parallel to the roof ridge.
To make the roof slope, frames are of different heights. Rafters are usually notched (called a birdsmouth) to fit over the purlins. Alternatively, purlins can have an angle planed on their top surface on which the rafters sit. Rafters are bolted to posts that they pass - to prevent the wind lifting the roof off.

**frames:
pitched roof
purlin frame**

ADVANTAGES

- Rafters can be formed into trusses to span large distances;
- Interesting internal spaces can be created;
- Rain will be 'shed' off a pitched roof;
- There is a wide choice of finishes.

DISADVANTAGES

- Space planning options are often limited by the roof shape;
- Fitting of rafters is difficult;
- More material is used and it is more complex to build than a flat roof.

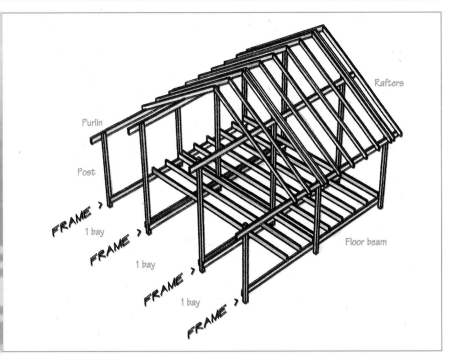

Purlin

Post

FRAME
1 bay

FRAME
1 bay

FRAME
1 bay

FRAME

Rafters

Floor beam

Above: Purlin frames to form one-, two- and three-bay structures.

Below: Three-bay purlin -framed house at C.A.T.

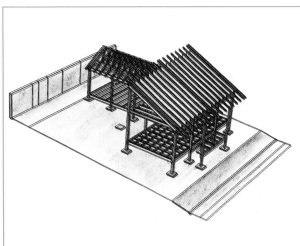

Left: a 'monopitch' roof structure.

frames: pitched roof principal rafter frame

A principal rafter is the name given to an inclined beam that supports the secondary timbers (purlins). It follows the profile of a pitched roof. Principal rafter frames are at right angles to the roof slope.

The decision on whether to use purlin frames or principal rafter frames depends mainly on the shape of the building - long thin ones will often have cross frames with principal rafters, squarer buildings may have purlin frames.

Right: *Principal rafter frames - perpendicular to the ridge.*

Below: *Three types of principal rafter and cross frames.*

ADVANTAGES
- Principal rafters can be formed into trusses to span large distances;
- Interesting internal spaces can be created;
- All difficult angled cuts are performed when laying out frames;
- Secondary timbers (purlins) are easier to fit than rafters;
- There is a wide choice of finishes.

DISADVANTAGES
- Planning options are often limited by the roof shape;
- More material is used and it is more complex to build than a flat roof.

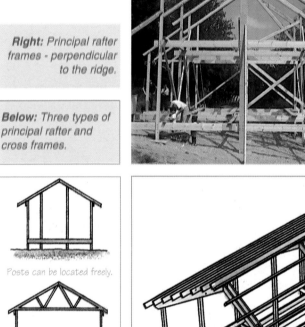

Posts can be located freely.

Trusses can be incorporated in the frame for wide spans

Principal rafter frames can also be portal frames - efficient against wind loads

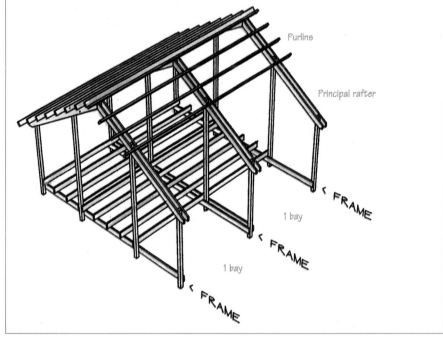

Purlins

Principal rafter

< FRAME

1 bay

< FRAME

1 bay

< FRAME

Whatever the frame type, it is usual in Segal Method buildings to have frames that reach all the way from foundation to roof - this is called 'balloon framing'. Unless posts are jointed ('scarfed'), the height of a frame is limited to the longest length of timber available - around 7 metres.

**frames:
balloon framing**

ADVANTAGES
- The frame is assembled flat on the ground;
- The frame is raised in one operation;
- The roof can be constructed at an early stage.

DISADVANTAGES
- Frames can be very heavy, requiring many helpers or mechanical aids;
- The height of posts is limited to the longest length of timber available;
- Two storeys maximum possible;
- Long, straight timber posts are costly.

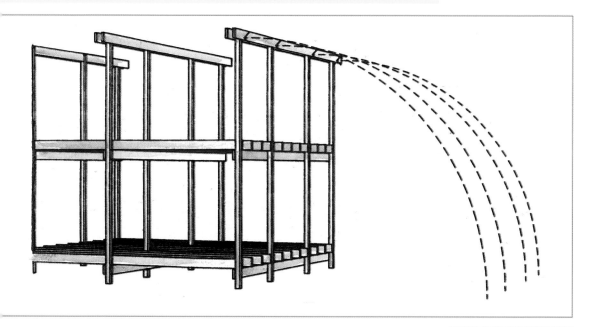

Above: *A whole two-storey frame-raising.*

frames: platform frame

Platform frames are one storey high. At each level, a platform floor is built, on which the next storey is raised. This technique has historically superseded balloon framing when long timbers have been scarce. Multi-storey buildings are possible - some mediaeval post and beam framed buildings are nine storeys high. At C.A.T. we have built a four storey station for the water balanced cliff railway.

ADVANTAGES
- Shorter, more readily available, cheaper timbers can be used;
- There is less weight to lift for each frame raising;
- Multi-storey buildings possible.

DISADVANTAGES
- Slower operation, as platforms have to be built at each level;
- Assembling and raising frames at high level can be hazardous.

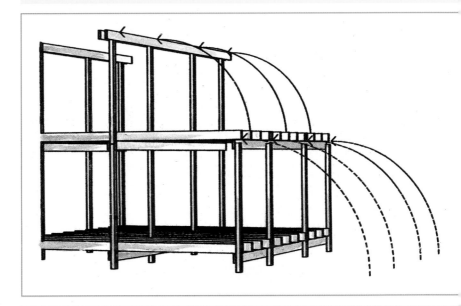

Above: *A frame raised on a platform (the top one) and a single storey frame.*

There is a huge range of possible solutions to the structural design of a post and beam building: timber species and grade, post shape, beam size and disposition, secondary timbers layout, cantilevers, bracing, trusses and so on - all of which affect the building layout, form and aesthetic. These structural notes only cover buildings based on right-angled grids that use squared posts. It is of course possible to have circular section timbers (whole trees) or pentagonal, hexagonal and octagonal grids and timbers, but jointing timbers at any angle other than 90 degrees requires much skill or purpose-made connectors. It is for this reason that all our furniture tends to be square; right-angled planning is universal and flexible.

Walter Segal used rectangular posts 50mm thick that fitted within the 50mm tartan grid space. The usual arrangement is that the post is at right-angles to the wall to avoid interference with wall panels. Although 50mm thick posts are slender, they are quite strong enough for most situations. Other designers have used post thicknesses of 75 and 100mm.

ADVANTAGES
- The post thickness can fit within the tartan grid;
- Deep rectangular posts can contribute to overall frame stiffness;
- It is easy to bolt a rectangular post to a rectangular beam.

DISADVANTAGES
- Load bearing capacity is limited by the slenderness of the post;
- Partitions have often to be cut to accommodate the depth;
- Free-standing ground floor posts will have to be protected from fire;
- It is difficult to bolt a rectangular post in the depth direction.

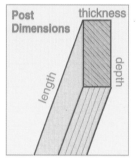

Post Dimensions

thickness, depth, length

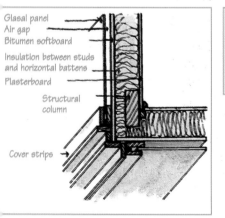

Glasal panel
Air gap
Bitumen softboard

Insulation between studs and horizontal battens

Plasterboard

Structural column

Cover strips →

Left: A rectangular post in a thick insulated wall.

Right: Walter Segal's original corner post construction, with less room for insulation.

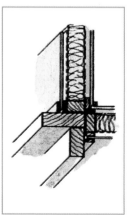

frame timbers and structure: square posts

Well-insulated buildings require much thicker walls than those originally designed by Walter Segal. These thicker wall constructions have sometimes led to the use of square posts, which are stronger for the same cross sectional area than rectangular posts. Some people prefer the look of square posts.

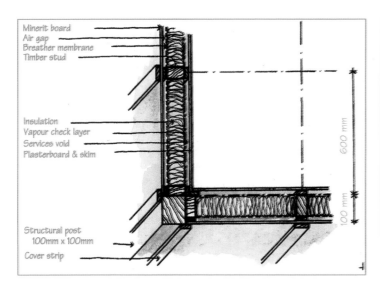

Minerit board
Air gap
Breather membrane
Timber stud

Insulation
Vapour check layer
Services void
Plasterboard & skim

Structural post
 100mm x 100mm
Cover strip

600 mm

100 mm

ADVANTAGES
- Square posts can take greater loads (for the same cross-sectional area);
- Beams can be housed into notches into posts for greater load bearing ;
- The posts fit within an irregular tartan grid with no partition-cutting;
- Freestanding ground floor posts are usually stout enough to require no fire protection.

DISADVANTAGES
- Cannot be used with a regular tartan grid.

A beam is the general name for any horizontal structural member (i.e. purlin, floor beam, rafter). Multiple beams supporting the floor, ceiling or flat roof are called joists. These can be sat on top of their supporting beams ('continuous'), or slung between them ('simply supported'). A simply supported beam spans between two points only.

All beams deflect (sag) slightly under their own self-weight and under the loads they are carrying. Beams have to be sized to keep deflection within acceptable limits - usually 1/300 of the span. Beams that deflect too much will not only look unsightly but will also be too 'springy'. This limit is usually the deciding factor in sizing a simply supported beam, rather than bending stress.

ADVANTAGES
- A first floor structure of joists fitted between two floor beams will be flat underneath, so that all partitions are the same height, making it simpler to build;
- If joists are set between the floor beams, the ground floor will be kept low to improve access.

DISADVANTAGES
- A greater depth of timber is needed for a simply supported beam than the equivalent 'continuous beam';
- Simply supported joists need bearers or hangers to fit them between their supporting beams;
- Joists cannot tie frames together.

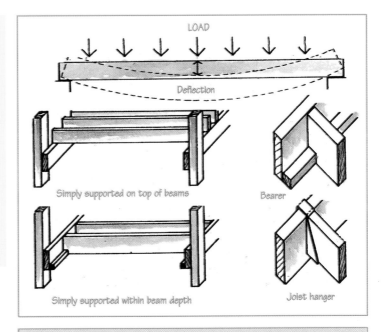

Above: A beam will deflect (sag) slightly. Joists can be carried on top of beams or slung between them.

frame timbers and structure: continuous beams

A 'continuous beam' is the name given to a beam (or purlin, joist or rafter) that has more than two supports. The bending in each bay will 'work against' the bending in the adjacent bays to structural advantage. Deflections - the limiting factor in simply supported beams - will be greatly reduced. The size limits are now set by the bending and shear (splitting) stresses induced at the supports.

ADVANTAGES

- Less timber depth is required than for the equivalent simply supported beam (or longer spans for the same depth);
- Joists can be bolted to posts they pass to tie the whole structure together;
- Much reduced deflections (springiness or sag in the middle of a span);
- It is easier to fix continuous joists, as they just sit on top of the floor beams.

DISADVANTAGES

- To act as one long beam, lengths of timber will have to be adequately 'scarfed' together;
- Joists must be 'thickened' (planed to all the same depth) to avoid an uneven floor;
- As joists run over the top of floor beams, these will project below the first floor;
- Thus wall partitions beneath joists will be taller than those beneath floor beams;
- The ground floor will be high off the ground, which may involve a lot of steps or a long ramp for access.

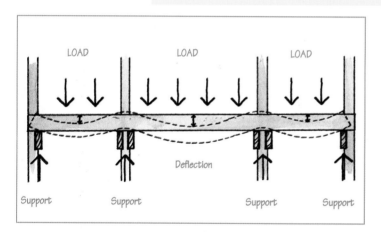

Above: Bending at the points of support will reduce bending at mid-span.

A cantilever is where a beam passes beyond its support. It is most frequently used for bay windows, balconies, steps and roof overhangs. As with the continuous beam there is structural advantage in using a cantilever - load on the end of the cantilever will tend to 'unbend' the main span.

frame timbers and structure: cantilever

ADVANTAGES

- A building with cantilevers will require fewer posts and foundations;
- Longer main spans are possible due to the 'unbending' effect;
- Cantilevers can provide overhangs to keep the post feet dry.

DISADVANTAGES

- If all the floor is cantilevered out from the post line, it is difficult to provide adequate wind-bracing (braces should fit between posts).

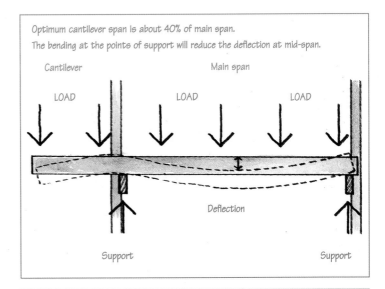

Optimum cantilever span is about 40% of main span.
The bending at the points of support will reduce the deflection at mid-span.

Cantilever Main span

LOAD LOAD LOAD

Deflection

Support Support

Above: *A cantilevered beam.*

**frame timbers
and structure:
knee brace**

Large beam spans and cantilevers can be propped by knee braces. These braces can also be used to give wind-bracing, by forming a triangle with the post and beam. The horizontal thrust from the knee brace needs to be countered either by very stout posts or by another, opposing brace. If there is no space under the building for knee braces, they can be included within the structure of a wall.

ADVANTAGES
- A building with braced overhangs will require fewer posts and foundations;
- On steep slopes, very long posts can be avoided;
- The extra brace supports result in smaller section beams (or longer spans);
- Overhangs can protect the post feet.

DISADVANTAGES
- Frames can be unwieldy to raise, as there are fewer posts to get people around;
- Overhangs supported by braces will always sag a little as the timber dries out and slack in the joints is taken up.

Left: A knee brace supporting a cantilevered bay.

Below: A knee brace can be positioned in a wall.

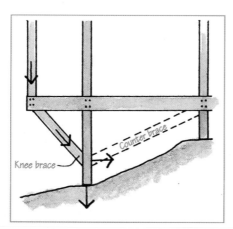

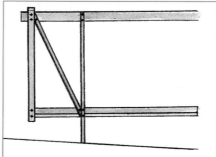

Above: *Huge overhangs are possible with knee braces, as shown on the Maldwyn Nursery and Family Centre, Newtown, Powys.*

Simple timber beams are economic for normal domestic buildings, but if large spans are required (more than about 4.2 metres) then special beams can be made which combine different materials to attain higher strength.

A ply web beam, in particular, is a very efficient use of materials - the equivalent steel I-beam requires fifteen times as much energy to make it.

ADVANTAGES
- Allows the creation of large spaces with no posts;
- High-performance beams can be made from lower quality materials.

DISADVANTAGES
- Composite beams will generally be heavy and awkward to raise.
- Transporting large beams is costly and awkward.

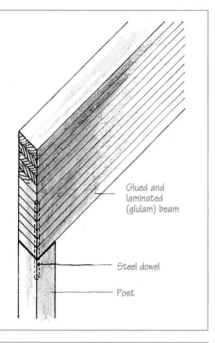

Glued and laminated (glulam) beam

Steel dowel

Post

Left: *A glulam beam is made from small strips of timber glued together (in a factory), rather like plywood. The combination of all these pieces yields a stronger beam than just solid timber. Very long and large beams can be manufactured, as the size is not dependent on tree size.*

Below Left: *A ply-web beam is a combination of timber and plywood formed into the familiar I shape seen in steel beams. Ply-web beams are extremely efficient, light and economical, but rather deep (giving reduced headroom). The pieces are held together by glue and nails and the beams can be made on site.*

Below: *Flitch-plate beams consist of a sandwich of two timber beams with a filling of steel plate, all bolted together. They are heavy and awkward but can span large distances with little depth.*

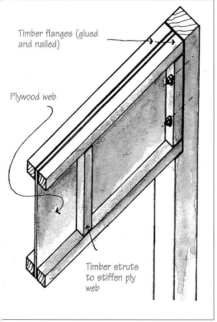

Timber flanges (glued and nailed)

Plywood web

Timber struts to stiffen ply web

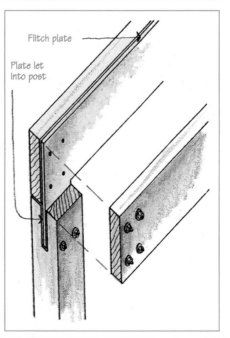

Flitch plate

Plate let into post

frame timbers and structure: trusses

A truss is a lattice beam made of small section timbers connected in triangles. The traditional way to span large distances in timber, many truss shapes have been devised. Trusses can be made up on site using only hand tools, but need careful calculation and equally careful construction.

ADVANTAGES
• Large spaces, free of posts, can be created.

DISADVANTAGES
• Trusses can be complicated to construct and heavy to raise.

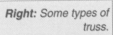

Right: Some types of truss.

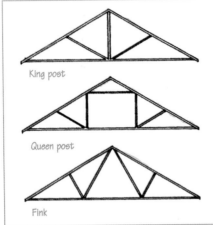

King post

Queen post

Fink

Above: Truss supporting the ridge of a roof in the community room at the Maldwyn Nursery and Family Centre, Newtown. Powys.

Top Right: Roof trusses spanning seven metres at the nursery room at Maldwyn Nursery and Family Centre, Newtown, Powys.

Bottom Right: Pitch-pine roof trusses at the Centre for Alternative Technology, Mid-Wales.

Jointing of timbers in a post and beam frame is critical - loads are transferred from the secondary members (joists and rafters) to the beams and thence by a joint to the posts and down to the foundations. Very often, the limit to a beam's span is not whether it will break, or bend too much, but whether the connecting joint with the post can take the load. The joint must be simple enough to be made on site using hand-held tools.

A bolt acts as a sort of peg on which the beam is hung. The size and number of bolts is determined by the load to be taken and by the grade of timber. The steel bolt itself is far stronger than the timber around it - the limit will be the crushing strength of the timber. Adequate timber must be left around the bolt to prevent splitting. This determines their spacing from each other and the edge of the timber. The bolt must be a snug fit into its hole, which is cut using a high quality auger bit. Large washers (3 times bolt diameter) should be used to prevent over-enthusiastic tightening pulling the bolt head through the timber.

If loads are too high for plain bolts (as in a truss) then toothed or split-ring washers can be used; in a normal post and beam joint there is little advantage, being difficult to fit and requiring special tools.

ADVANTAGES
- Bolting timbers together is simple and fast.

DISADVANTAGES
- Very accurate drilling is required;
- The load capacity of a bolted joint is limited by post width (this favours deep rectangular posts);
- Large bolts are expensive;
- Single beams impart eccentric loading on the post;
- Bolt heads get in the way of subsequent work;
- As the timber shrinks on drying, the nuts slacken.

Below Left: *A simple bolted joint; the letters indicate critical dimensions necessary to prevent the bolt splitting the timber.*

Below Right *A toothed plate connector for bolting joints.*

Below: *Drilling timbers for a bolted joint.*

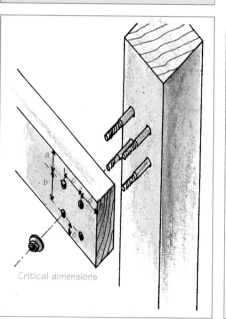

Critical dimensions

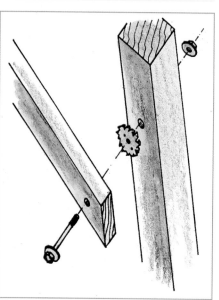

frame joints: housed

Part of the post can be notched away to fully or partly 'house' the beam. Most of the load is transferred directly from the beam to the post - the notch giving a far greater bearing area than that available from bolts. Some load is taken by the light bolts or coach-screws holding the joint together. Housings are formed by hand saw and chisel, or by many passes of a circular saw and then chisel-work.

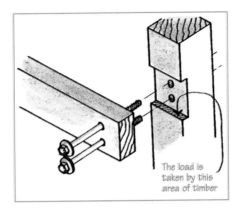

The load is taken by this area of timber

ADVANTAGES
- Higher loads (from longer spans/fewer posts) can be taken compared to just bolting;
- Will be cheaper than the equivalent bolted joints;
- Loading is not as eccentric as bolted joints;
- There are fewer bolt heads to get in the way and there is more choice over where they are positioned.

DISADVANTAGES
- Housing is a slower and more skilled process than drilling and bolting;
- Posts will have to be stout enough to allow timber to be removed for the housing.

frame joints: half-lap

A half-lap is similar to the housed joint, but a notch is taken out of both timbers and the two housings put together. They are rarely used for post/beam connections as the beam would have timber taken away at just the point it needs to be at its strongest. They are mostly used for cross-braces where the bracing timbers are required to be within a wall thickness.

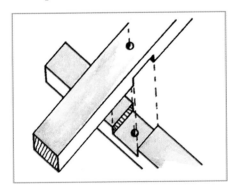

ADVANTAGES
- Two timbers can be joined in the same plane.

DISADVANTAGES
- The timbers are rather weak at the joint;
- Careful and accurate work is required.

The mortice and tenon is the traditional carpentry joint, where part of a post (tenon) is fitted into a hole in the beam (mortice) and held in position by a timber peg. This joint can carry very high loads as the beam has plenty of timber to bear on - although it can be easily broken if there is any sideways or upward load. Making a mortice and tenon joint is a skilled job, made easier by the advent of mobile chain morticers.

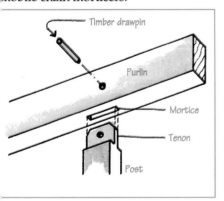

ADVANTAGES
- It is a low-tech joint;
- Only one material is used;
- It is very strong when transferring loads from beam to post;
- Beams and posts can be in the same plane.

DISADVANTAGES
- Careful accurate work is required;
- The joint cannot take much load in the upward direction (which may result from wind lift on roofs).

frame joints: scarf joints

As buildings tend to be longer than available timbers, many ways have been devised to join timbers end-to-end. The position of such a joint (called a scarf) along a beam is critical, as the joint will be weaker than the beams and cannot take bending. The principle is best imagined as one beam resting on the cantilevered end of another.

ADVANTAGES
- Scarf joints allow advantage to be taken from continuous beam action;
- Long beams can be made from short, cheaper timbers.

DISADVANTAGES
- The joints have to be made and positioned accurately.

Right: Simple 45° scarf, used for joists.

Middle Right: Stopped splayed scarf, used for single beams.

Bottom Right: Butt and filler, used for double beams.

Below: Posts also can be scarfed, as well as joists and beams.

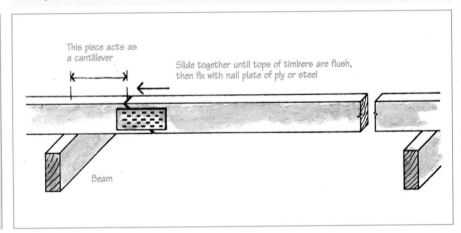

This piece acts as a cantilever

Slide together until tops of timbers are flush, then fix with nail plate of ply or steel

Beam

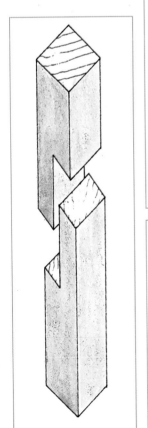

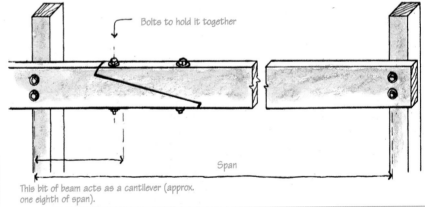

Bolts to hold it together

Span

This bit of beam acts as a cantilever (approx. one eighth of span).

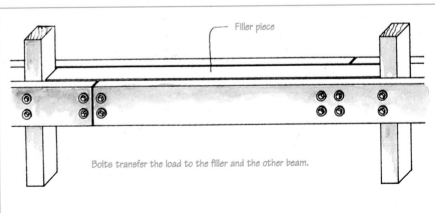

Filler piece

Bolts transfer the load to the filler and the other beam.

When wind hits the side of the building and blows over the roof, horizontal and vertical forces result (called racking forces) that have to be resisted and transferred safely down to the foundations. This is done by making parts of the building stiff; a rigid box that cannot be distorted. Floors will act as rigid plates as they are fully boarded; walls and roofs likewise can be boarded (called sheathing on a wall and sarking on a roof), or can have triangular braces added.

A brace is an element introduced to triangulate and therefore stiffen a structure. A triangle cannot be distorted without bending one of its three sides. Thus if the timber members are sturdy enough the triangle formed will be perfectly rigid. In a timber post and beam frame, braces transfer horizontal wind load from a beam down to the base of a post. As it is best to use a timber brace in compression, there must be a brace in both possible wind directions, usually in the form of a St. Andrew's cross in the plane of the frame. Bracing should also be provided in the other direction, between frames. Often, to stiffen it, a roof has nailed cross-bracing on the underside of its rafters/purlins.

ADVANTAGES
• Once bracing members, roof and floors are in place, the structure is complete and walls can be added or taken away at will.

DISADVANTAGES
• On highly-glazed, open-plan buildings, it is sometimes difficult to find blank walls to put cross braces in;
• It is awkward fitting walling materials around the sloping brace members.

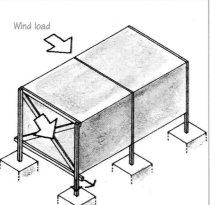

Far Left: Bracing prevents a building 'racking'.

Left: Crossed wind braces on the low-energy house at the Centre for Alternative Technology, Machynlleth.

Left: Two types of cross brace.

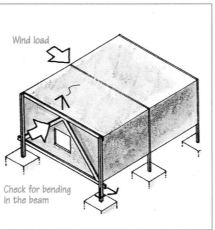

Wind load

Wind load

Check for bending in the beam

frame wind bracing: panel sheathing

A boarded floor or roof will act as a rigid panel. Similarly, if the wall construction requires fixed panel materials to contain insulation and provide the finish, these panels can also provide the required bracing (called racking resistance). This sheathing has to be nailed at close centres and will not therefore be easily re-usable if walls are altered. If sheathing alone does not provide enough racking resistance, braces can be introduced, angled between the wall studs.

ADVANTAGES
- Materials that have to be part of the wall anyway can have the dual function of providing bracing.

DISADVANTAGES
- Walls cannot be removed without recalculating racking resistance;
- The building is not fully braced until all walls are in position (temporary bracing must remain);
- Walls are not easily relocatable.

Below: Panel sheathing.

Bottom: Braces.

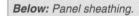

Top: Fibreboard sheathing on stud walls. As well as providing racking resistance, the sheathing contains loose-fill insulation and a weather-tight enclosure is quickly formed. This example is from the Bristol self build pilot scheme.

Above: Tongued-and-grooved fibreboard sheathing, seen here on the Fusions Jameen Self Build in Lewisham, South London.

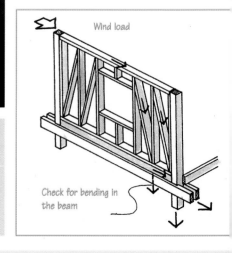

Wind load

Wind load

Check for bending in the beam

Once the structural frame has been squared and braced, work can begin on roof construction. This will consist of timber members spanning between the roof beams, clad in various layers of materials.

Walter Segal likened the external skin of a building to human clothing:
• The raincoat - to keep us dry;
• The woolly jumper - to keep us warm;
• The vest - to give comfort next to the skin.

In buildings, the skins also have to be stiff to take the snow and wind loads and to take shelves and pictures. The constructions in this section show different arrangements of raincoats, jumpers and vests for roof, walls and floor. As with clothing, the best constructions are those that 'breathe' - the Gore-tex raincoat rather than the PVC one.

Human activity creates water-vapour (breathing, sweating, washing, cooking) which must be allowed to escape from the building without causing damage through condensation. The external skin should be designed to control water-vapour so that condensation does not occur deep within the structure, and yet enable it to 'breathe'. This is done by having:
• An external rain-screen that protects the construction, but which is well ventilated;
• Insulation that allows vapour to pass easily through it;
• An internal finish that is more resistant to water-vapour than the external finish (see 'breathing' walls, page 71).

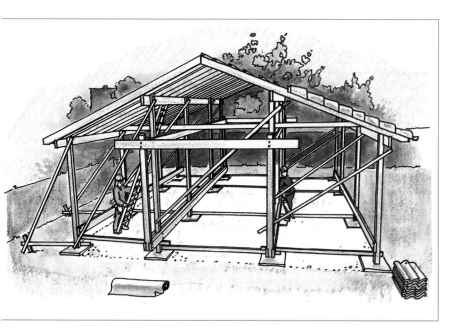

external skin: ventilated 'cold' roof

Walter Segal designed a flat roof construction that avoided the pitfalls - and leaks - of a conventional flat roof. By laying the roof membrane loosely over the deck, expansion movements could take place without tearing the membrane. Pebble ballast and the edge trim prevented the membrane from blowing off; see illustration below.

To prevent condensation on roof timbers, there must be good ventilation on the cold side of the insulation. In a conventional pitched roof this ventilation is provided by the loft space; where the ceiling line follows the roof, a ventilated airspace is provided (the Building Regulations call for 50mm).

If you prefer a sloping roof, conventional pitched roof tiles and slates provide a safe, well ventilated rain-screen. Two types of ventilated pitched roof are also illustrated opposite.

To achieve a high level of insulation within the roof, composite rafters can be used to give extra depth. Illustrated in two forms right, their advantage is that they save on timber costs and provide better insulation.

Right Top: Ventilated flat roof construction.

Bottom: *Traditional ventilated loft-space construction. Arrows show the circulation of air.*

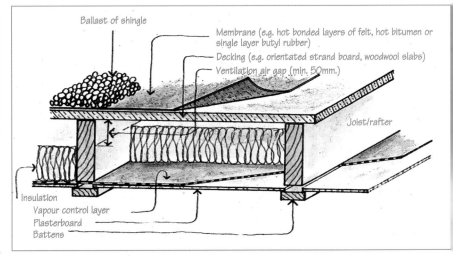

Ballast of shingle

Membrane (e.g. hot bonded layers of felt, hot bitumen or single layer butyl rubber)

Decking (e.g. orientated strand board, woodwool slabs)

Ventilation air gap (min. 50mm.)

Joist/rafter

Insulation
Vapour control layer
Plasterboard
Battens

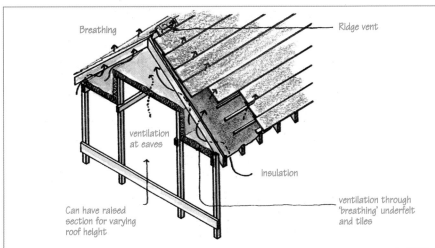

Breathing

Ridge vent

ventilation at eaves

insulation

Can have raised section for varying roof height

ventilation through 'breathing' underfelt and tiles

ADVANTAGES

- Any type of insulation can be used (which can be low-cost and benign);
- Can be a 'breathing' construction.

DISADVANTAGES

- Good ventilation is necessary to prevent condensation;
- Some timbers on the cold side of the insulation could be subject to condensation;
- Construction can be slow and elaborate;
- Where the ceiling line follows the roof pitch, rafters have to be deep to contain a reasonable insulation thickness and ventilation space.

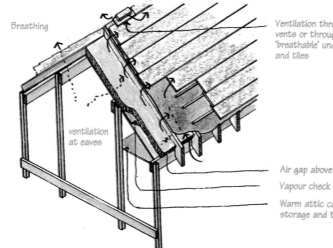

Breathing

ventilation at eaves

Ventilation through ridge vents or through 'breathable' underfelt and tiles

Air gap above

Vapour check layer, if required

Warm attic can be formed for storage and tanks

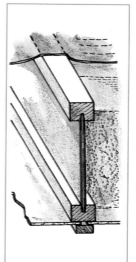

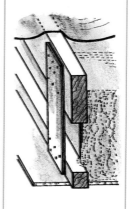

Above: *Ventilated roof, with ceiling line of room following the interior of the rafters.*

Right Top: *Manufactured composite deep rafter.*

Right Below: *Composite deep rafter made from two slender timbers plated together.*

external skin: unventilated 'warm' roof

If the insulation is placed outside of the construction, the supporting structure underneath is 'warm'. A good vapour barrier has to be installed above the structure to prevent condensation occurring within the insulation. If waterproof insulation is used then only the waterproof layer is needed - below the insulation.

Right Top: *Unventilated warm pitched roof.*

Centre: *Unventilated warm flat roof.*

Bottom: *Unventilated 'upside down' flat roof with waterproof insulation.*

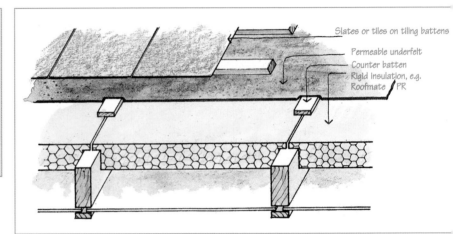

Slates or tiles on tiling battens
Permeable underfelt
Counter batten
Rigid insulation, e.g.
Roofmate PR

ADVANTAGES
- Structure is on the warm side of the insulation and therefore protected from condensation;
- Construction is fast;
- A 'beamed' ceiling can be shown to aesthetic advantage.

DISADVANTAGES
- Ecologically undesirable rigid insulation is required;
- A warm roof depends on a perfect vapour control layer;
- Upside-down roof requires even more expensive and undesirable insulation;
- A 'breathing' construction is not possible.

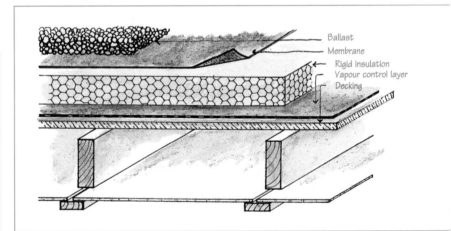

Ballast
Membrane
Rigid insulation
Vapour control layer
Decking

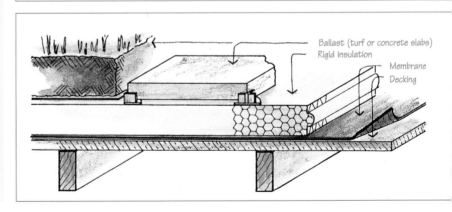

Ballast (turf or concrete slabs)
Rigid insulation
Membrane
Decking

With the roof covered, the floors are constructed - under shelter. Floor joists are laid out in the modular grid positions and flooring (floorboards or sheets) temporarily laid so that work can proceed on the external walls. Once the walls enclose the building, services can start to be installed and the floors can be insulated and decked.

A Segal Method building normally has the ground floor raised above the ground. It therefore has to be insulated to the same standard as any other element; usually by laying insulation on supporting panels fixed between the joists. If these panels are made from a material of low vapour resistance the whole construction will 'breathe'. Water and electrical services can be laid within the insulation if preferred (but this restricts later access).

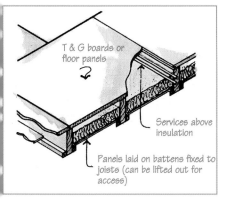

T & G boards or floor panels

Services above insulation

Panels laid on battens fixed to joists (can be lifted out for access)

ADVANTAGES
- Suspended floors are cheaper on sloping sites than solid floors;
- Frames are well 'tied together';
- They are easy and cheap to 'superinsulate';
- Services can easily be accommodated;
- They are 'breathing' constructions;
- A useful undercroft can be created.

DISADVANTAGES
- The high floor level requires long access ramps;
- If heavy loadings are imposed (e.g. in a public building) many posts and foundations will be required.

external skin: solid ground floor

In some situations such as large public buildings, heavy workshops and garages a solid ground floor may be desirable. Access to the building is easier as the floor level will be very near to the ground level. As there are no longer any ground floor beams to tie the framing together, posts will have to be bolted down to the foundation to prevent sideways movement. Insulation, under the floor finish, has to be able to take weight and must be protected by a damp-proof membrane and vapour barrier.

ADVANTAGES	DISADVANTAGES
• High loads can be taken;	• Expensive rigid insulation materials are required;
• Ramped access is easier than for a suspended floor;	• A solid floor uses lots of concrete (see *Materials* section);
• A clean, flat work area is created for building work;	• 'Breathing' construction is not possible;
• On flat sites, this may be a cheaper construction;	• Setting-out has to be more accurate;
• There is less heat loss from a solid floor, as the earth provides some insulation.	• Posts have to be bolted down;
	• It is difficult to incorporate services;
	• More earth-moving and materials moving is required - which is all hard work and messy.

Below: *Solid ground floor. Posts and solid plates must be bolted/tied down to the concrete slab to make a complete structure.*

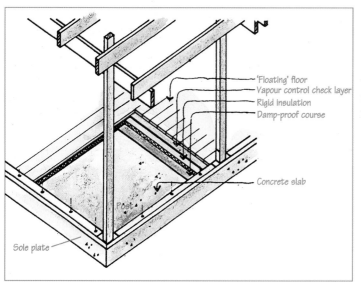

'Floating' floor
Vapour control check layer
Rigid insulation
Damp-proof course

Concrete slab

Post

Sole plate

Above: *A suspended ground floor (see previous page).*

Once the roof has been covered, and floor joists and some temporary flooring have been laid, the building becomes a covered workshop and the external walls can be constructed.

Walter Segal's original external walls were simple and low-cost. They comprised a fibrous-cement sheet 'raincoat'; a rigid woodwool/cement slab 'jumper'; a sheet of painted plasterboard 'vest'. To build 'superinsulated', draughtproof walls using ecologically sound materials is more difficult - some of the simplicity is lost. However, such walls are still low-cost compared to a conventional masonry building.

Human activity (breathing, perspiring, cooking, washing etc.) creates water vapour. This leads to an increase in the moisture content of the air inside buildings and can lead to condensation forming on cold surfaces, such as windows or poorly-insulated walls. In a well-insulated building this condensation could take place deep inside the wall - which, in the case of timber-frame, could lead to wood rot. Normally, however, this is prevented from happening by a vapour control layer which is placed on the warm side of the insulation.

In conventional timber-frame walls this layer has to be highly impermeable to water vapour, as there is no way for vapour to escape once inside the wall. This can lead to the internal climate being either too humid or too dry, as there is no water vapour exchange between inside and outside. To overcome these shortcomings, the 'breathing' wall is designed in such a way that there is a slow, diffusive exchange - water vapour can slowly escape through the wall without condensation occuring; and can migrate into a building if the internal climate is too dry. Materials are chosen to give a higher vapour resistance inside the wall than out - usually in the ratio of 5 to 1.

Timber and timber products (including cellulose insulation) are hygroscopic - that is they can absorb excess atmospheric water during periods of high humidity and let it out again during dry periods. This all helps to temper the internal environment and increase comfort.

external skin: rigid panelled walls

Better insulated versions of Walter Segal's original rigid panel wall have been built, but there is difficulty in finding a suitable material with better insulating properties that is also rigid enough and environmentally benign. Such walls are still inherently draughty.

For unheated spaces (porches, workshops, garages, conservatories) this type of wall is ideal.

ADVANTAGES
- They are simple and fast to build, and readily demountable.

DISADVANTAGES
- Rigid insulation materials are expensive and can be environmentally unsound;
- Such walls may be draughty.

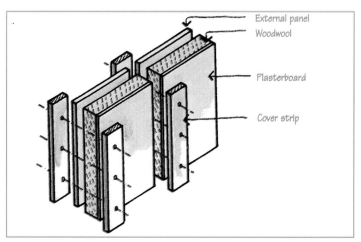

External panel
Woodwool

Plasterboard

Cover strip

Above: *External wall panels of woodwool, foam insulation and plasterboard, seen while extending Ken Atkins' house in Lewisham.*

external skin: spaced panelled walls

It is possible to build two simple 'Walter Segal type' walls spaced apart, and fill the void with loose fill insulation.

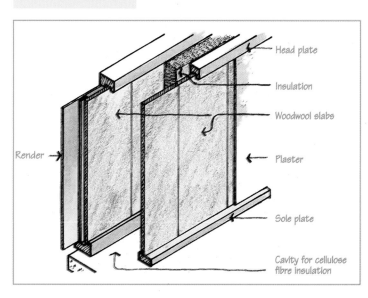

Head plate

Insulation

Woodwool slabs

Render

Plaster

Sole plate

Cavity for cellulose fibre insulation

ADVANTAGES
- Low cost, environmentally benign insulation can be used;
- Good sound-proofing.

DISADVANTAGES
- The two layers of woodwool slab make a very heavy and thick construction.

Left: *Spaced panels: woodwool slabs span from the sole plate on the floor to the head plate, forming a wide cavity, which is filled with cellulose fibres. Birmingham Ecology Centre.*

Studs are vertical timbers set a modular distance apart, to which sheet materials are attached. Low-cost insulation can then be used between the studs. Stud walls can be made 'on the flat' inside the building and then raised into position between the posts, or 'stick-built' piece by piece. The external cladding rain-screen should be spaced off from the insulation to provide a ventilated airspace.

external skin: stud walls

ADVANTAGES

- Studs provide a fast and simple way of quickly enclosing the building;
- Any insulation material can be used;
- The construction will tend to be less draughty than the simple panel type;
- There is a wide choice of sheathing materials, many of which can also serve as structural wind bracing.

DISADVANTAGES

- Studding at close centres (every 600mm) uses a lot of timber - the studs would probably be strong enough to hold up the building, thus duplicating the post and beam structure;
- Walls are not easily relocatable.

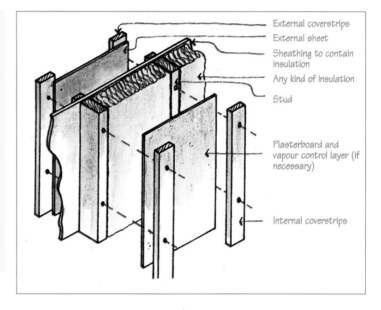

External coverstrips

External sheet

Sheathing to contain insulation

Any kind of insulation

Stud

Plasterboard and vapour control layer (if necessary)

Internal coverstrips

external skin: spaced stud walls

In a conventional stud wall, heat passes through the stud at a much faster rate than through the insulating material. Timber is also much more expensive than insulation. The spaced stud uses two small-section studs spaced apart, so forming a 'thermal break'.

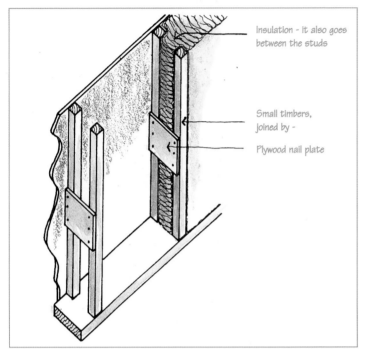

Insulation - it also goes between the studs

Small timbers, joined by -

Plywood nail plate

ADVANTAGES
- Less timber is used than with the equivalent solid stud walls;
- Spaced studs are better insulated than solid timber studs.

DISADVANTAGES
- Construction is slower and more fiddly than the equivalent solid stud wall.

Right: Spaced studs and spaced rafters seen at a self build house in St. Harmon, Radnorshire.

A stud wall can be built in layers using small timbers fixed at right angles to each other - for example, 75 x 50 vertical studs with 50 x 50 horizontal rails.

ADVANTAGES
- Thermally 'broken' studwork gives a better U-value than the equivalent solid stud;
- Provides a zone for the easy fixing of wind-bracing;
- Lighter pieces of timber are easier to handle;
- Smaller timber sections are cheaper.

DISADVANTAGES
- An extra process is introduced;
- Such a wall uses the same amount of timber as conventional solid stud walls.

Below: This self build house at Hope Wharf, London shows counterstuds - 75x50 verticals and 50x50 rails.

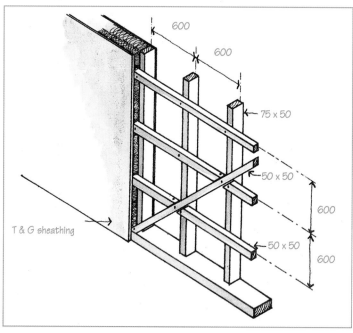

T & G sheathing

600
600
75 x 50
50 x 50
600
50 x 50
600

external skin: windows and doors

Walter Segal's original windows were very simple and low-cost, consisting of just sheets of glass sliding in an aluminium angle, the whole held by timber beads in a timber lining. Such windows can be of any size and avoid dependence on a manufacturer. They are, however, draughty and fiddly to construct.

external skin: manufactured window and door units

High-performance softwood windows and doors are readily available that are properly draught-stripped and can incorporate advanced glazing units. They can be obtained in the common modular size of 600mm (and multiples -1200, 1800, 2400mm). High-performance softwood Scandinavian windows, increasingly used in low-energy buildings, are made-to-measure.

ADVANTAGES
- High-performance windows and doors are available that are well draught-sealed and fitted with robust catches;
- Ready-made windows are fast to install, and some can be ordered factory-glazed.

DISADVANTAGES
- Good quality windows and doors are expensive;
- Delivery times can be long and uncertain.

Left: Off-the-shelf 600mm modular windows and doors were used at this self build house in Telford, Shropshire.

Fixed windows using double or triple-glazing can be built in-situ. High-performance opening windows and doors can be incorporated into this fixed glazing. Such an arrangement is very adaptable and can provide a variety of shapes and sizes, with the expensive opening unit incorporated where necessary.

external skin: windows and doors built *in situ*

ADVANTAGES
- Considerably lower cost than all bought-in units;
- The designer is not limited to manufacturer's styles and sizes.

DISADVANTAGES
- Slower and more complex to construct.

Below: In situ *fixed windows incorporating bought-in opening lights in Calthorpe Community Centre, King's Cross, London.*

external skin: bay windows

Below: Bay window hung off roof (Left) and full height bay cantilevered off main floor (Right).

A floor or roof can easily be cantilevered out to support a bay or oriel window - for a window seat or bed alcove.

A bay window will admit extra daylight and perhaps catch sunlight coming at an angle to the building face. It will make a building bigger without increasing the foundation's 'footprint'.

ADVANTAGES
• Spatial delight;
• Extra space and light can be added without extra posts and foundations.

DISADVANTAGES
• They are time-consuming to build;
• They have a high surface area which adds to the building's heat loss.

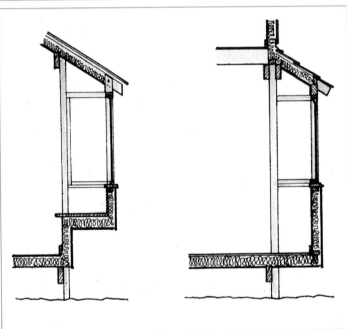

Above Left: Bay window at the self build scheme in Lewisham.

Above Right: Bay window at houses in Camden, London.

Top Right: Window seat in a house in Sheffield.

Right: A bay window at the Greenwich Self Build Co-op, London.

lerestory lights is the name given to high level windows, often above the main oof line, that can usefully bring daylight and sunshine into a deep building.

ADVANTAGES
* They can improve daylighting in deep buildings.

DISADVANTAGES
* High level windows are troublesome to clean.

Far Left: Clerestory lights in Calthorpe Community Centre, King's Cross, London.

Left: Triple-glazed ridge light supported by a trussed ridge beam in an office at the Centre for Alternative Technology, Machynlleth, Wales.

Below: Clerestory lights at the London Wildlife Trust, London.

**external skin:
conservatories
and porches**

Unheated conservatories and porches form a 'buffer' between the heated areas of a building and the outside, thus reducing heat loss. They are easy to construct using the simple, common-sense construction of the Segal Method, providing low-cost living space that can usefully extend a building for much of the year.

ADVANTAGES
- They provide low-cost intermediate zones beween inside and out, which have energy benefits (buffering).

DISADVANTAGES
- Conservatories can become so popular that they are used as normal rooms and wastefully heated during the winter;
- They can also interrupt views and ventilation for inner rooms.

Top Left: Conservatory under a turf roof at Surrey Docks Farm, London.

Left: Two-storey conservatory at Glasgow Garden Festival House.

Top Right: Integral conservatory at a house at Ffos-y-ffin, Dyfed.

Above: Conservatory linking three buildings at Maldwyn Nursery and Family Centre, Newtown, Powys.

With post and beam construction it is simple to extend the frames, floor and roof to form a verandah. For times when the weather is warm but wet, a verandah can form an extra outside room.

external skin: verandahs

ADVANTAGES
- Verandahs are low-cost, sheltered outside rooms which provide an intermediate zone between 'out' and 'in'.

DISADVANTAGES
- On windy sites they will not give much protection.

Far Left: *A verandah at the Bristol self build pilot scheme.*

Left : *Glazed verandah linking two buildings in the residential courses' accommodation, Centre for Alternative Technology.*

Bottom Left: *Approach ramp, porch and deck, Hop Farm Visitors' Centre, Kent.*

Below: *Deck, pergola and verandah on a Herefordshire workshop.*

Bottom: *Deck, pergola and verandah at Surrey Docks Farm, London.*

internal walls and services

Once the roof, floor and external walls create a weathertight space, internal walls (partitions) and ceilings can be constructed. Door frames are usually made up on site and incorporated into the walls.

The electrical service installation will be brought up from the floor - to power and lighting outlets and to switches in the partitions and ceiling.

These are usually made of a rigid 50mm woodwool slab covered both sides with plasterboard. The assembly is held in place by timber coverstrips screwed from either side into 50 x 50mm blocks or into a stud between the woodwool slabs. The walls are simple to construct and relocatable. Wiring can be run in the 50 x 50 space between panels.

ADVANTAGES

- They are fast to construct and easily relocatable;
- It is easy to fix shelves to the coverstrips.·

DISADVANTAGES

- The sound insulation between adjacent rooms is poor, due to air gaps in the all-dry construction;
- Not everybody likes the striped effect of the vertical battens.

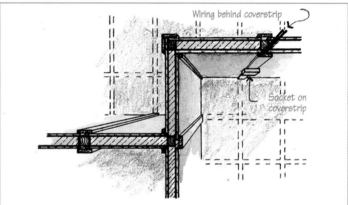

Wiring behind coverstrip

Socket on coverstrip

Left: *Rigid panel partition with coverstrips and plasterboard.*

internal walls: stud walls

This is the conventional way to construct a timber wall, usually built on a centreline grid. Timber studs span from floor to ceiling and have plasterboard sheets fixed to them. Coverstrips can be used to clamp the materials together or the wall can be finished in plaster. The spaces between the studs can be filled with absorbent material to improve sound insulation.

ADVANTAGES
- Better sound insulation is possible;
- There is a choice of coverstrips or plaster finish.

DISADVANTAGES
- Not such an easily relocatable wall as the panel type.

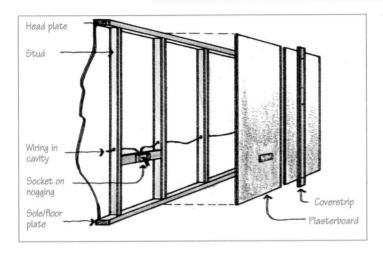

Head plate
Stud
Wiring in cavity
Socket on nogging
Sole/floor plate
Coverstrip
Plasterboard

internal walls: service voids

A good deal of time and money is spent on installing services (hot and cold water, central heating, electrics, telephone). These service runs should preferably be accessible and not buried in insulation. The dry assembly building techniques of a Segal Method building makes for easier servicing.

ADVANTAGES
- Easier installation and maintenance of services.

DISADVANTAGES
- Involves some extra cost and work.

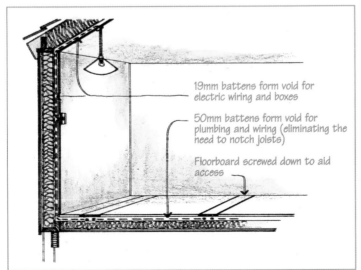

19mm battens form void for electric wiring and boxes

50mm battens form void for plumbing and wiring (eliminating the need to notch joists)

Floorboard screwed down to aid access

Above: *Electrical wiring in the first floor 'void' with 'drops' at the partitions.*

Stairs (internal) and steps (up to the ground floor from the outside) can be constructed simply by fixing treads to hangers suspended from joists or beams - thus the complicated joinery of a conventional stair, with its housed strings, is avoided. Treads can be stiffened by 'risers' screwed to the underside which also reduce the gap between treads (to stop little people falling through). Internal stairs must be glued as well as screwed to prevent creaking. External seats, balconies and internal shelving can all be hung off the structure in the same way.

ADVANTAGES
- Can be built at lower cost than conventional stairs;
- A great variety is possible;
- Easy to make.

DISADVANTAGES
- The stairs are made of a great many small parts which have to be maintained;
- Internal stairs will be creaky if not all the joints are glued.

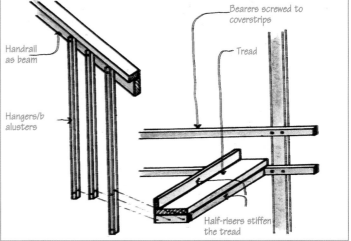

Bearers screwed to coverstrips

Handrail as beam

Tread

Hangers/b alusters

Half-risers stiffen the tread

Left: A hanging staircase at the Glasgow Garden Festival house.

THE SERVICES include heating, electrical appliances, ventilation, water and sewage. They should end up as energy-efficient and as environmentally-friendly as possible, as well as providing the kind of comfort you expect.

Space and water heating

Solar heating has the lowest running costs and is the most environmentally sound of all options. Ideally you have already designed your building to make maximum use of the sun's heat for space heating, as suggested on pages 18-21. Proper management of solar heat (called 'passive solar') together with hi gh levels of insulation and control of ventilation can save up to 90% of space heating bills. We also recommended installing solar water heating panels, which will provide about 40% of your water heating along the UK's latitude. Any other heating system should properly be seen as a back-up or top-up to these.

Wood is relatively clean to burn as long as it is well seasoned. If the trees are replaced by replanting there is no net effect on global CO_2 levels.

Natural gas is one of the cheapest fuels and is the least polluting fossil fuel. Its transportation by an efficient national distribution system yields an ecological advantage as well as low costs.

Liquefied Petroleum Gas (LPG), often known as propane or

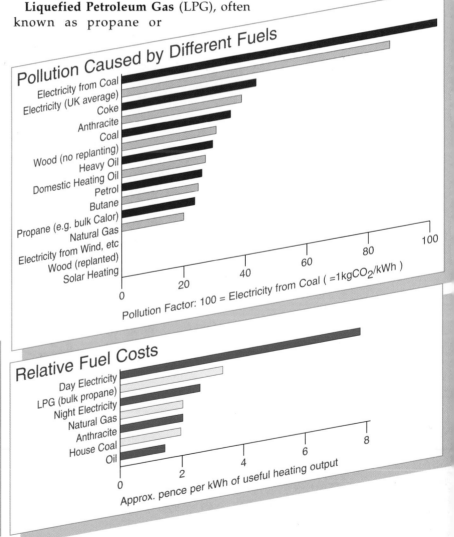

Pollution Caused by Different Fuels

Electricity from Coal
Electricity (UK average)
Coke
Anthracite
Coal
Wood (no replanting)
Heavy Oil
Domestic Heating Oil
Petrol
Butane
Propane (e.g. bulk Calor)
Natural Gas
Electricity from Wind, etc
Wood (replanted)
Solar Heating

0   20   40   60   80   100

Pollution Factor: 100 = Electricity from Coal (=1kgCO$_2$/kWh)

Relative Fuel Costs

Day Electricity
LPG (bulk propane)
Night Electricity
Natural Gas
Anthracite
House Coal
Oil

0   2   4   6   8

Approx. pence per kWh of useful heating output

Right: Figures from the Association for Environment-Conscious Building, showing that renewable energy causes no net pollution, and electricity from coal the most pollution. Electricity is by far the most inefficient of fuels, because of the conversion factor.

butane, is a by-product of making petroleum from crude oil. If natural gas is not available in your area, it is the cleanest fossil fuel you can use, but dearer than gas or oil because of the transport costs.

Oil is popular because of its low price, though this is always subject to fluctuation. More polluting than gas in terms of CO_2 emissions, but less so than coal, its transportation by sea carries a risk of marine pollution in the event of spillage.

Coal (including coke and anthracite), unless burned under carefully controlled conditions, is very polluting. It produces high levels of carbon dioxide and sulphur dioxide. Nowadays its main contribution to household heating lies in the large-scale production of electricity.

Electricity (unless it comes from a renewable source) is the most polluting fuel, owing to the high pollution costs of coal, gas or nuclear power, and the inefficiency of the conversion process. It is also the most expensive.

Boilers: This is a crucial choice, as the efficiency of the boiler (in converting fuel to heat) is the main variable in the efficiency of the whole system. The majority of central heating boilers on the market today are 60-70% efficient, but there are some variations:

'Combi' (or combination) boilers, which heat the water on demand, dispense with the need for a storage tank, and therefore eliminate the heat losses associated with storage and long pipe runs. There may be some restriction in the rate of flow with this type of boiler.

Condensing boilers: These boilers are designed to save most of the heat which normally escapes with the flue gases, by inserting one or two heat exchangers in the flue. Developed originally for commercial and industrial premises, there have been a few teething problems associated with their adaptation for domestic use. For these boilers to function efficiently, the temperature of the return water needs to be lower than would normally be necessary. This can be achieved by oversizing the radiators, but this approach still contains an element of trial and error. Nevertheless, they are recommended by the Building Research Establishment and claim an efficiency of 90-95%. They are available for use with oil, natural gas or LPG.

Space heating is usually delivered by water-filled radiators. However, when building from scratch, it is worth considering installing underfloor heating, which works at lower temperatures and is therefore a good match for condensing boilers. It is in general a more efficient method of heat delivery and eliminates cold spots that can occur, e.g. around windows.

Heating controls are another important element of a heating system. There are programmers which switch the boiler on and off at pre-set times, and thermostats which adjust the amount of heat the boiler puts out, according to actual and desired temperatures.

Thermostatic radiator valves improve the efficiency of the whole system and allow individual rooms to be maintained at different temperatures.

There are also advanced controls and programmers now available (e.g. by Dataterm) which give a more constant controlled temperature (plus or minus half a degree Centigrade from the set temperature). They can also 'learn' the heat-up time of the building, and monitor the outdoor temperature, and then incorporate this information into achieving the desired temperature at the pre-set time.

services

Electrics

Although we are looking to minimise the amount of electricity used in the home, we do need a certain amount for lighting, TVs and other appliances.

Lighting: An ecological approach to lighting a building could result in considerable reductions in the amount of fuel used. A major consideration of the design process should be to maximise the daylighting of the interior, thus reducing the use of electric lights. Large south-facing windows, roof lights, and a shallow plan form all help to achieve this effect.

Conventional tungsten-filament, incandescent bulbs are extremely inefficient, generating far more heat than light.

Energy efficient light bulbs, known as Compact Fluorescents (or CFs) are efficient, and widely available and, although they are more expensive to buy, each one pays back its original cost by three to four times. They are used with electronic ballasts which eliminate the annoying flicker associated with the old fluorescent tubes. Modern CFs give a 'warm' yellow light which mimics that given by incandescent bulbs. Full-spectrum CFs are also available, which mimic daylight.

Unfortunately, CFs cannot be used with dimmer switches.

Electro-magnetic radiation

There is a growing concern among proponents of healthy buildings about the possible harmful effects of electro-magnetic radiation (EMR). Electro-magnetic fields surround electrical appliances even when not in use, as long as they are plugged into the mains. People are often unaware of cables buried in walls, or the possible effect of an appliance on the other side of a partition wall. Of particular concern is people's exposure to EMR when asleep.

Copper shielded cables, which screen out EMR, are available, but at great expense.

Demand switches (from Natural Therapeutics) can be fitted at the consumer unit, and if there is no demand on a particular circuit, all power to that circuit is cut off. Alternatively you can just switch off the mains every night and rely on battery-operated clocks and radios. Appliances which need a constant supply, e.g. the fridge or boiler, have to be on a separate, dedicated circuit.

Separate spur circuits, as opposed to a ring main, are more easily controlled and isolated, and do not have the effect of completely surrounding a room with buried cables. Water pipes and radiators are also a source of EMR. Sleep away from these if possible.

Avoid siting your house under or near overhead high-voltage power lines.

Below: One energy-saving light bulb lasts as long as eight ordinary bulbs, costing therefore one third the amount. It uses one fifth of the electrical power. By using one you therefore spend just over a third of what you would have done using conventional bulbs. The return on the investment in the higher price of the low-energy bulb is about 30% over three years - better than any current high interest account. Similar levels of returns on investments apply in most cases of spending on energy efficiency measures.

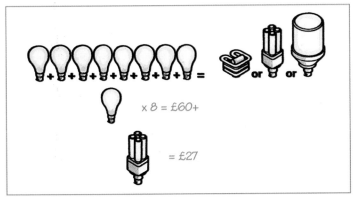

x 8 = £60+

= £27

Water

Only 5-10% of our water supply needs to be of drinking water standard. Yet a lot of resources go into treating and purifying all our water to this standard (supposedly). The other 90% of our water needs could be met by other means.

Rainwater, stored in butts, can be used for the garden (but beware of lead flashings on roofs as a possible contaminant). Grey water (waste from sinks and baths), can be passed through a grease and soap interceptor, and reused for non-drinking and non-cooking purposes.

We also need to be aware of the sheer quantity of water we use, not only because it is metered, or when there is a drought, but because increased demand leads to more flooding of valleys for reservoirs. Appliances such as washing machines and dish washers are very wasteful of water, as are conventional toilet cisterns. Low-flush toilet cisterns are available which use only one third of the normal amount of water. Fitting these, and using showers instead of baths would reduce our water consumption by 35%.

You may wish to remove impurities from your water supply by using a water filter. It is important to choose one designed to filter out the particular pollutants in your supply. You should be able to obtain a water analysis from your local water company. Fit a plumbed-in filter if possible - it is more effective against a greater number of pollutants. Jugs need their filters changing regularly or they can attract bacteria and create a concentration of pollutants.

Be sure to use lead-free solder on all water pipes.

Ventilation

We need to ventilate our buildings, in order to replace stale, smelly air with fresh air. However because ventilation, in general, is accompanied by heat loss, we also need to be able to control it.

Traditionally, ventilation was achieved by a fairly uncontrolled infiltration of air round ill-fitting doors and windows. As buildings become more tightly sealed, controlled ventilation becomes even more important.

One way of ensuring this is to install a mechanical ventilation system with a heat recovery facility. This extracts stale, moist air from the kitchen and bathroom and transfers its heat to fresh, incoming air. It is relatively easily installed as part of the building process, but it does need a tightly sealed building in order to work effectively. It doesn't actually save on primary energy as electricity is needed to drive the fans which operate the system.

Natural ventilation relies on the stack effect traditionally supplied by open fireplaces and chimneys. Differences in temperature and pressure between inside and outside will always tend to draw fresh air up through the house. This tendency can be assisted by specially provided flues or ducts rising to an outlet in the roof and operated by humidity sensors. This system can be supplemented with extractor fans in the kitchen and bathroom, but these fans need their own fresh air supply.

Trickle vents, fitted as standard on most window frames, allow for a small, constant amount of ventilation, without the draughts normally associated with opening a window.

A Green Guide to Building Materials

IN THE PROCESS of designing a building, certain choices about materials are made very early on (e.g. whether to build with timber or masonry). Other choices occur at virtually every stage of construction, right down to internal finishes. These opportunities are special to the self builder, who is able to choose environmentally good materials. Buildings composed of such products will not necessarily cost any more than those built with other products. Therefore, when specifying any building material, an awareness of 'ecological costs' is helpful. This term is generally taken to cover three main areas of environmental damage.

1. The amount of fossil fuels (coal, oil and gas) used to produce, process and transport a given material. This is called 'embodied energy' and can be measured in kilowatt hours (kWh) per tonne or cubic metre (see table overleaf). These fuels come from a finite source, but because of their present abundance, they are used in a profligate way to provide us all with a very cheap energy source.

2. The pollution of air, ground and water, generated by the production process, usage and final disposal of a given material. The atmospheric pollution caused by the burning of fossil fuels is of particular concern. This causes global warming, acid rain and ozone depletion, and can be broadly measured in the amount of carbon dioxide released (kg CO_2/kWh). Global warming, with its likely consequence of severe climatic change, poses probably the biggest threat to life on earth as we know it. Other pollutants created by the burning of fossil fuels include sulphur dioxide, nitrogen oxides and carbon monoxide.

3. The use of non-renewable resources (other than fossil fuels) such as ores, rock, clay, sand and aggregates, used to produce metals, bricks and tiles, cement and concrete, lime and plaster. Although these raw materials may seem to be abundant, even infinite, the huge quantities demanded by the modern building industry cannot be extracted without significant environmental damage. Indeed, limestone, with its myriad uses, is being so intensively quarried in areas like the Yorkshire Dales and the Peak District that entire ranges of hills are at risk. With any extraction of minerals from the earth's surface comes destruction of natural habitats and widespread scarring of the landscape. Moreover, as easily accessible reserves of raw materials diminish, hitherto unexploited areas of land become threatened with 'development'.

In general, for any given material, the closer to its natural state it is, and the less processed it is, the better it will be in environmental terms. It is the high-energy, high-temperature production processes of many metals and plastics which carry a high 'ecological cost'. In some cases we may decide that it is a cost worth paying, particularly where no other material can be substituted, (e.g.

MATERIAL	kWh/TONNE	kWh/m³
Bricks	860	1,462
Clay tiles	800	1,520
Local slates	200	540
Single layer roof membrane	45,000	47,000
Concrete 1:3:6	275	600
Lightweight Blocks	500	600
Natural sand/aggregate	30	45
Sand/cement render	277	400
Plaster/plasterboard	890	900
Steel	13,200	103,000
Copper	15,000	133,000
Aluminium	27,000	75,600
Timber (imported softwood)	1,450	754
Timber (local airdried)	200	110
Timber (local green oak)	200	220
Glass	9,200	23,000
Plastics	45,000	47,000
Plastic insulation		1,125
Mineral wool		230
Cellulose insulation		133

Right: *The energy content of various building materials: These figures should be used very loosely as they are estimated from different sources, including our own observations. However, they do highlight some interesting differences, such as the advantage of a slate roof (860) over a membrane (18,800) that will be used in a turf roof construction. The approximate energy costs of a low rise masonry house of 100m2 is 115,000kWh. A timber frame building of 50% homegrown costs 57,000kWh. So timber frame buldings have the lowest energy costs.*

Below: *Cost and efficiency of main fuel types for space heating purposes. As with the table on page 88, electricity shows up as a fuel of poor efficiency in conversion from its primary source.*

FUEL	PRICE	EFFICIENCY OF HEATING PLANT	COST per kWh (USEFUL)	PRIMARY kWh FOR ONE USEFUL kWh
GAS				
Normal Boiler	45.9p/Therm	70%	2.20p	1.56
Condensing		90%	1.70p	1.22
ELECTRICITY				
On-peak	7.64p/kWh	100%	7.64p	3.70
Economy7 Day	8.09p/kWh	100%	8.09p	3.70
Economy7 Night	2.60p/kWh	75%	3.46p	4.90
OIL 35sec (domestic variety)	13.0p/litre	70%	1.78p	1.56
SOLID FUEL				
Coal	£100/tonne	45%	2.67p	2.27
Anthracite	£150/tonne	65%	2.54p	1.85
Coalflow pearls	£110/tonne	65%	2.03p	1.85
LPG bulk tank				
Normal Boiler	16.0p/litre	70%	3.20p	1.56
Condensing		90%	2.91p	1.22
WOOD air-dried				
in woodstove	£30/tonne	65%	1.84p	very small

copper wiring). There is often a trade-off to be made between the ecological cost of a material, and the contribution made by that material to the overall energy efficiency of a building (e.g. in the case of insulation). However, an environmentally responsible approach must mean that we at least examine these costs, and try to minimise the use of materials which carry a huge hidden debt in terms of resources and pollution. Using the analogy of the earth's resources as a 'pot of gold', we should be investing it wisely and living prudently off the interest generated, rather than squandering the capital in a short space of time.

For a preliminary evaluation of the ecological costs of building materials, it is useful to assess each one according to the following criteria:

1. Is it renewable? To be truly renewable, a material should have no net impact on the earth's resources. Such materials are the products of living organisms which use the sun's energy for their growth and development. In building, the most common renewable material is timber which has been harvested on a sustainable basis and replaced by replanting. This includes timber products such as boards and sheets, as well as paper. Labour can also be seen as a renewable resource and this perspective serves to moderate the appetite for 'low maintenance' products, usually made of metal or plastic.

2. Is it reusable? If a material can be reused without re-processing, e.g. re-cutting a piece of glass or timber, this obviously represents an energy saving, and in this sense it is better than using either new or recycled materials. The potential for future reuse can be incorporated into current building practice e.g. using 'soft' low-cement mortar, which enables bricks and blocks to be reused. The same potential exists in bolting rather than welding steelwork. There is a movement among ecologically conscious designers to 'design for disassembly', leading to eventual reuse or recycling, as well as facilitating repairs and adaptation.

3. Is it recyclable or biodegradable? The ecological costs of many metals, of some plastics and of glass are mitigated by their potential for being recycled. There are of course energy costs involved in recycling, which makes 'reuse where possible' the best option. Biodegradable materials such as timber are in effect naturally recycled. We need to become more aware of all materials as potentially part of an interdependent cycle of use and reuse. At present, the building industry is one of the most waste-generating industries there is.

4. Is it energy-efficient? This relates to the energy-efficiency (or otherwise) of the production process, as well as to the efficiency of the primary fuel used in that process. Where large amounts of energy are used, it is worth asking whether any provision for heat recovery has been made. Or, if the primary fuel is electricity (very polluting in production and inefficient in conversion), can renewable alternatives be explored? For example, the high cost (financial as well as environmental) of aluminium manufacture has led some producers to use hydro power (though this can involve the flooding of valleys). Or again, there are several brick manufacturers in the U.K. who use a proportion of bio-gas (30-40%) in the fuel they use to fire their bricks. As building consumers become more demanding of 'green' credentials, such energy-saving innovations in methods of production are likely to become a big selling point.

5. Is it locally grown or produced? This criterion, where successfully applied, would greatly reduce the transport element of the embodied energy cost, as well as stimulating local economies and encouraging a more diverse pattern of production.

6. Is it durable? This criterion reduces the need for frequent replacement, itself a waste of resources. In ecological terms it is almost always better to choose a high quality, long life product (which does not necessarily mean paying more in the long term). Ease of maintenance and repair, which increases the useful life of

Above: Homegrown oak and recycled pitch-pine structural frame, joists and floor, with homegrown Douglas fir and larch rafters and sarking, on the top railway station at the Centre for Alternative Technology, Machynlleth.

a product, is also worth checking on before buying.

7. Is it healthy? Does it have any adverse effects on the building workers or eventual occupants? Possible sources of toxins and irritants common to many modern homes include:

- off-gassing from plastics, resins, rubbers and foams used in insulation and furnishings;
- formaldehyde vapour from the glues used in plywood and chipboard, as well as in some insulation materials;
- fibres from asbestos or mineral fibre insulation;
- vapours from timber treatment and dust from treated timber;
- vapours from cleaning materials, solvents, paints and varnishes;
- lead in old paints released through paint stripping;
- radon, a form of naturally occurring radiation.

Again, benefits and costs need to be weighed carefully. A small amount of toxic material in an inaccessible place (e.g. lead flashings on a roof) may pose very little risk compared with a lot of plastics and synthetic finishes internally with which you will come into close daily contact.

One of the main difficulties in choosing environmentally-benign materials is the lack of reliable and specific information, particularly where the consumer needs it most of all - at the point of purchase. Suppliers often simply don't know the ecological or health impact of the products they sell, and manufacturers generally fail to provide such information. A trustworthy and comprehensive system of labelling, coded symbols and background data on all manufactured goods is sorely needed.

It is outside the scope of this book to examine every building material for its environmental impact. However, below we have a closer look at the particular materials you are likely to come across when designing and building a timber frame house.

Timber

Timber scores highly on all the above criteria and is therefore always the material of first choice for us, but timber comes from various sources and it is crucial to be aware of this.

Imported softwood

This is what most builders merchants and timber yards stock as standard.

Some is from well managed forests. Indeed some forest industries (e.g. in Scandinavia) place great emphasis on their replanting programmes. Grown slowly at high latitudes, imported softwood is denser and therefore stronger than homegrown. Some of this timber still comes from old growth forests in North America and should be avoided at all costs.

If it is impossible to ascertain the ecological pedigree of timber supplies and if you cannot obtain homegrown, Scandinavian timbers are the most likely to be sustainably produced, in the sense that felled trees are replanted. True sustainability, in the sense of recreating mixed habitats and conditions for biodiversity, remains elusive and extremely hard to verify.

The heartwood of Douglas fir and larch (imported or homegrown) is classified as 'semi-durable'. Detailed correctly, such timber will need no chemical preservatives.

Secondhand timber should be used whenever possible as it is well seasoned and saves on energy costs. Secondhand pitch pine is a beautiful structural timber - but it is expensive when resawn and converted to manageable sizes.

Most of the embodied energy in timber comes from transport energy costs, so the closer the timber is grown to the building site, the better.

Homegrown softwood

For most domestic sized structural timber, homegrown softwood is quite strong enough. Indeed, using larger sections of slightly weaker timber results in a more solid, less springy building.

Above: A self build house using a local green oak frame with traditional carpentry joints at Penybontfawr, Montgomeryshire.

As well as having less embodied energy than its imported equivalent, the use of homegrown timber encourages rural industries. The homegrown timber industry is not as well organised as that of the importers. It has been used principally to supply fencing stakes and other low value products and it is generally not so used to supplying the quality or quantity required for timber framing. However, some firms are gearing up to meet these requirements (see Resource Guide). The costs are similar to imported softwood, but the embodied energy is typically only one seventh (see table).

By specifying large section softwood, the self builder is creating a demand for large trees, which can only be grown in well-managed, thinned plantations. A thinned mature forest has much more value as a wildlife habitat than the dense forestry/clear-felled regime that results from the demands of the paper pulp and chipboard industry.

Homegrown hardwood

This is the traditional material of timber framing (mostly oak and sweet chestnut). Very strong, heavy and durable, these timbers are usually worked green (unseasoned). Green oak is fairly expensive - probably twice the price of structural softwood - but as the timber frame component is only about 5% of the total building costs, the extra expenditure is well within many budgets.

Timber certification

It is a problem obtaining timber from sustainable sources. Even timber from Scandinavia isn't necessarily trouble-free. Despite only having 1-2% of old growth forests left, amidst a sea of commercially-managed forest, Norway, Sweden and Finland are still felling natural forests for timber. Happily there are an increasing number of timber merchants and retailers committed to using only timber from well-managed forests, that don't cause environmental and social damage. At the moment it is difficult to separate this timber from a mass of other products claiming that timber used comes from 'sustainable' sources. But a group of environmentalists, foresters and retailers set up the Forest Stewardship Council in October 1993. The FSC will act as an umbrella organisation for timber certification bodies around the world. These will, in turn, certify that timber from subscribing bodies meets the social and environmental standards set by the FSC. The system acts a bit like certification of organic food, and indeed in the UK one of the first certification bodies to set up a timber scheme is the Soil Association. At the moment it seems likely that certified timber could get a bigger share of the market in a few years. In Britain stores such as B&Q, Texas Homecare, Do-It-All and Boots are committed to using certified timber. Watch out for FSC labels appearing on timber over the next few years and choose where possible.

Generally, bolted joints are not used, as oak contains tannic acid (natural preservative) which gradually attacks the galvanised steel. The greatest practical drawback to using green oak or sweet chestnut is the weight. Machinery will usually have to be hired to raise the frames.

Small section green oak - say 100 mm depth, and 1.8 to 2.4m long - is fairly cheap and adds value to thinnings which would otherwise be used for firewood. Products from waste hardwoods, such as block and strip flooring and panelling, are being developed by organisations such as Coed Cymru (see the Resource Guide). This sort of demand will slowly improve and encourage the planting of our native hardwood forests, the most diverse and valuable wildlife habitats in Britain.

Tropical hardwoods

It is important to emphasise that there is currently no tropical hardwood that can be guaranteed to come from sustainable sources. Many claims that are made to this effect do not bear examination. The International Timber Trades Organisation estimates that less than 0.2% of the world's tropical rainforests is being managed on a sustainable basis. The best advice is: don't use it at all. The environmental effects of wholesale logging are disastrous: soil erosion, flooding, loss of innumerable wildlife habitats, fruits and medicines, conversion of a vast carbon reservoir into CO_2.

In most tropical regions, deforestation is driven principally not by export demand but by domestic needs for timber and fuel, and to create new farmland. India is for instance the largest producer of tropical timber in the world, 91% of which is used for fuel. In 1989, fifty million cubic metres of hardwood were extracted from the Brazilian Amazon. 48 million of these were used in the home market. To date 12% of the Amazon rainforest has been destroyed, but as the forests of south east Asia become worked out, that figure will change dramatically.

In theory, the greater value that is added by exports could be used to finance more environmentally sensitive forms of development. A highly discriminating export market could stimulate the establishment of well managed plantations and sustainable patterns of growth - and, paradoxically, help save the remaining tropical forests. In the long term, then, we should develop inspection and certification schemes, such as the one currently being worked on by the Soil Association. We should build up trading links with sustainable producers and make use of tropical timbers in a rational way.

In the short term, until such schemes are in place, it is best to avoid all tropical timbers, especially Brazilian mahogany, and the hardwood veneers which face most commonly available plywoods. If the colour is reddish brown - beware! You will have to ask specifically for oak - or birch-faced ply, for example - or order it from a large supplier who stocks many different sorts (see Resource Guide).

Timber treatment

A huge industry has grown up to protect from decay poor quality timber used inappropriately. Indeed for decades the timber treatment industry has both masked and thrived on inadequate seasoning of timber and poor design. By definition, timber treatment involves toxic chemicals, and even these provide only temporary protection. Long-term guarantees are often worthless.

Well seasoned timber, on the other hand, can cope with getting a bit wet sometimes - providing it can dry out again. A Segal Method building can generally 'breathe', i.e. air can circulate round external timbers and percolate through the structure. Special care must be taken with wall construction where timber members are enclosed within a cavity, particularly where (as in non-Segal buildings) the timbers cannot easily be inspected. If vapour barriers are used inappropriately, condensation trapped within the cavity can cause these timbers to rot. This whole area is discussed further under 'breathing walls' in the Construction section.

With external timber - structural and decorative - sunlight destroys (delignifies) the external surface of the timber which can then become porous and liable to water penetration. A wood stain or varnish can be used to prevent this happening.

One area that can cause concern is the base of the posts, which can remain damp. Although the damp proof course will reduce the amount of water drawn into the post endgrain, it is as well to protect this area further by inserting Borate rods at an angle into the post heart. Borax is a salt that has antiseptic properties, and, being soluble in water it will only start to work should there be a dampness problem. In spite of these precautions, should rot still occur in this area, it is relatively easy to identify and treat.

Much of the structural, rough sawn timber in stock at builders yards will already be treated, and you should state specifically if you want untreated timber. If you do decide that you need to use treated timber, then CCA (chrome, copper, arsenic) is one of the safest treatments. These elements combine chemically with the timber and have a low volatility, thus minimising the risk from inhalation.

All treated timber, including off-cuts and saw dust, should be treated as toxic waste and not burnt or inhaled.

There are three other types of building materials that are worth a closer examination in terms of their particular qualities and drawbacks. These are metals, plastics and cement. Although not used extensively in timber frame construction, they will occur in many different guises, and some basic information is necessary in order to assess them.

Metals

Metals are manufactured by quarrying or mining natural non-renewable ores and then smelting them with various additives at high temperatures. Little effort is made to exploit the potential for heat recovery within this industry. Many metals are recyclable, and especially where the production costs are high, this becomes financially worthwhile. Some metals are particularly toxic to humans, e.g. chromium and lead, and their use should be restricted as much as possible.

Iron and steel

Ecologically the most damaging effects of iron and steel production are the sheer quantity of raw materials consumed, and the large amount of energy used. The iron and steel industry has the highest energy usage of all the big industrial consumers. Historically, in Europe, coke replaced charcoal as the primary fuel used in the smelting process. However in other parts of the world today, charcoal is much in demand for smelting pig iron, and vast areas of the Amazonian rainforest are being felled to meet this demand.

The self builder will almost certainly make use of iron and steel, often with a zinc coating, for nails, screws and bolts, as well as radiators and many appliances. Stainless steel is made with the addition of 5% of chromium, whose manufacture produces several highly toxic by-products. However, its corrosion resistance increases the durability of the item, and makes it invaluable in certain applications, e.g. kitchen sinks and flue pipes. It is highly amenable to recycling.

Top: *Colour-coated profiled steel roof at Hope Wharf Self Build, Peckham, London.*

Middle: *Plain clay tile roofing on sheltered housing in Churt, Surrey.*

Bottom: *Glazed clay pantile roofing on a house in Mill Hill, London.*

Aluminium

Made from the very common ore, bauxite, this is nevertheless difficult to extract and consumes a great deal of energy in the production process, giving it the highest embodied energy content of all the products discussed here. It is, however, easily recycled, the process for which uses only 5% of the original energy cost (compared with steel's 30%). The self builder may come across aluminium as nails, particularly for roofing, or in the form of aluminium foil, as a vapour resistant backing for plasterboard. More wasteful uses of aluminium include window frames, ceiling tiles and profiled roofing sheets. The use of aluminium in cooking utensils and/or as a contaminant of drinking water has been associated with Alzheimer's disease.

Copper

Its main environmental drawback is the release of sulphur dioxide into the atmosphere during the smelting process. However it is invaluable in electrical wiring and is also commonly used in plumbing pipes (gas, water and heating), as well as in hot water tanks. There are plastic plumbing systems now on the market, which are a lot easier for the amateur to use, but they are more expensive and not necessarily better environmentally.

Lead

Due to its high toxicity, its use in water pipes and solder is being phased out. However it is a good material for roof flashings and valleys, as long as the run-off is not used for drinking or on the garden. It is present in much old paintwork, which should not be stripped by burning or dry sanding. Apart from roofing purposes, the self builder may use lead in thin weathering strips above and below window frames, and as the damp proof course under each post, but there are satisfactory alternatives available, e.g. Nuralite.

Plastics

A product of the petro-chemical industry, the ecological costs of plastics production are made worse by the problems of disposal. Most plastics will not biodegrade and are not easily recycled because of the complex mixture of compounds they contain. At present, 10% of all the refined oil that is produced goes to make plastics, but as our oil reserves are being depleted, alternatives are being found.

Plastics can also be made from sugar cane, slaughterhouse waste (already used for formaldehyde), casein, cellulose and rubber latex. For the moment, increased effort needs to go into developing single polymer plastics in pure form, (e.g. P.E.T. - polyethylene tetrachloride, instead of P.V.C. - polyvinyl chloride) and better facilities for recycling, or even energy-producing incineration, as a solution to non-degradable waste.

PVC is particularly polluting in its manufacture due to the inevitable leaks of chlorine gas. Highly corrosive and used as a poison gas during the first world war, chlorine is also a powerful ozone-destroyer.

The use of synthetic plastic fittings and surfaces, particularly in ill-ventilated areas, has been implicated in 'sick building syndrome'. However perhaps the most serious health risk it poses is the release of toxic gases during combustion. We should minimise the use of plastics in our internal furnishings and finishes, but the self builder will find that plastic water pipes and plastic-coated cable are unavoidable (although cables coated with chlorine-free plastic are available). Other items which are commonly specified in plastic can be obtained in other materials (e.g. metal gutters or clay drainpipes), but at greater expense.

Top Right: *Roofs of larch boarding and natural slate on the top station at the Centre for Alternative Technology, Mid-Wales.*

Above: *Turf roofs on the Diggers self build, Brighton.*

Cement

The basic ingredients are lime and clay, combined with varying quantities of silica, alumina, iron oxides and gypsum, heated together to 1500 degrees C. The high temperature is an indication of the large amount of energy required, and pollution is caused by the emissions of heavy metals (especially with high alumina cement) and oxides of sulphur. In the USA there is evidence that the cement industry is burning hazardous waste in its kilns - adding to the polluting effect of the production process - and then defending the practice as 'recycling'.

The quarrying of limestone for cement causes scarring of great tracts of countryside and, at certain times, a serious dust hazard in the locality. Concrete is not recyclable, although it can be reused as hardcore. In any event, the process of demolition involves literally smashing or blowing it to pieces, at great energy and expense. The main health risks associated with using cement come from inhalation of the dry dust, which can cause silicosis, or skin contact with wet cement which, though painless at the time, can cause severe burns. A recent study of 600 cement workers in Kent found a much higher rate of stomach cancer than would normally have been expected, thought to be due to chromates - a trace impurity in all cements. When mixing concrete, various additives are available, such as calcium chloride, to speed up setting times or to make the mixture more plastic and workable, and these can cause dermatitis and eczema.

Having said all this, it is difficult to imagine a modern building industry without the use of some cement. The real problem here lies in the excessive specification and use of concrete and other cement based products. One of the great advantages of post and beam buildings is that they only have concrete foundations where they are actually needed - at the foot of each post. This leads to environmental savings by minimising the requirement for cement, and financial savings by obviating the need for large scale earth moving and mechanical digging. Once the self builder has cast the small foundation pads, there is no need to handle wet cement again throughout the whole building process. Cement products such as roofing tiles, fibre reinforced cement sheets for external walls, or woodwool slabs may well be used but do not present a significant hazard.

We will now examine particular materials, as they occur in different parts of the building.

Roof finishes
Membranes

These are flexible waterproof sheeting materials for flat and low pitch roofs. They are laid on a flat deck, such as plywood sheets on rafters. By their impervious nature, they cannot 'breathe', but some are low cost and make for fast construction.

a) Bitumen and felt: vegetable and mineral fibre-based rolls of felt are glued together in three layers by hot or cold bitumen. Hot bitumen laying is a messy and dangerous business best left to professionals. The materials are relatively benign. If loose-laid as in the Segal Method, it should be long-lasting, providing it is well protected from sun and thermal movement. However, on turf roofed buildings couch grass roots can penetrate the felt.

b) Single layer plastic or synthetic rubber: can be made up in the factory to the correct size and laid like a tablecloth. Upstands for rooflights and flues are easily formed by gluing or welding with a hot air gun. It should be protected with geotextile layers from accidental puncture. The material is petro-chemical based, so it has a high energy content. It is long-lasting, providing it is protected from the sun. (Ordinary polythene degrades within a year in sunlight.) It is invulnerable to couch grass roots and is a high quality membrane for a turf roof. Examples of this product on the market are butyl rubber and Hypalon (see Resource Guide).

Rigid sheets

These may be profiled (corrugated) sheets of fibre-cement or metal, laid on purlins with a minimum pitch of about 15°. Profiled sheeting is generally low-cost and fast. Flat sheets of zinc or other malleable metals can be used, with standing seams (a very skilled and expensive job).

a) Fibre cement corrugated sheet: low cost material whose appearance improves with age (moss, etc). Brittle, it needs handling with care, and should not be stood or walked on without boards to spread the weight. It is, of course, a product of the cement industry. It is less prone to condensation than metal sheets, but the construction should still include a breathable sarking felt, e.g.

Tyvek or Corovin, to protect the building from drips.

b) Bitumen fibre sheeting: made from bitumen reinforced with vegetable fibres, it may need more frequent support than fibre cement sheet and has a shorter life. Marketed as Onduline.

c) Galvanised and plastic-coated steel: the main problem is condensation occurring on the underside in cold weather. Industrial buildings usually use 'warm' construction with a vapour barrier. You can use a condensation catching breather felt. As with all galvanised products, the zinc content of the coating may cause disposal problems.

d) Aluminium sheeting: as with c), but has a very high embodied energy content.

e) Plastics sheeting: for roof glazing. The 'twin-walled' type is light weight with good thermal properties but has a high energy content and will go translucent and brittle. You cannot see through it.

f) Glass: high energy material, but with a long life and made from a plentiful resource. An inert, 'healthy' material, it is recyclable and available as toughened laminated or wired glass, for high impact resistance and safe shattering.

Above: Thatch on a floating Segal Method building at the Norfolk Naturalist Trust, Ranworth Broad.

Tiles

These provide the ideal of a 'breathing' rain screen.

a) Natural stone and slate: low energy materials requiring a high degree of skill to lay. Very long lasting but relatively expensive. There is a lot of Spanish (Iberian) slate on the market at the moment which is cheaper, but poorer quality, than Welsh or Cumbrian slate.

b) Fibre reinforced cement (or artificial) slate: a cheap alternative to real slate, they have the appearance of unnaturally flat slates of uniform thickness. Due to their tendency to delaminate, they usually have an extra bottom fixing of a copper rivet. Originally made from asbestos, the fibres are now cellulose. More sophisticated versions strive for an appearance similar to natural slate and use slate dust bonded with an epoxy resin.

c) Concrete: fairly low energy product of the cement industry. Interlocking tiles are available. Heavier than slate or clay tiles, they require stronger and stronger rafters. Glazed tiles are very long lasting.

d) Clay: higher energy content, but from a less polluting industry than c). Interlocking types available. Glazed tiles are very long lasting.

e) Timber shingles (cut) or shakes (split) of durable species (oak or cedar): not long lasting, but they are from a renewable resource, although many cedar shingles come from non-sustainable sources. They need a steep pitch.

f) Timber boarding: not long lasting but from a renewable resource. The boarding acts as a screen against sun and rain and depends on a good underfelt sarking.

Below: A flowering meadow on a house.

Other

a) Turf or sod: not a waterproof finish in itself, but a good protector of membrane roofs. Holds snow well and reduces wind chill, otherwise it has little insulating value. Also able to bear flowers, a turf roof's appeal lies in it replacing the greenery now covered by the building. It is also a good place to sit.

b) Thatch: a renewable, low energy material and a good insulator, it can gracefully cover complicated roof shapes. But it is expensive and needs skilled work to install.

Above: Greening the city: turf roof on a self built community centre, Mill Lane, London.

Right: Turf roof and twinwall polycarbonate roofed conservatory on a staff house at the Centre for Alternative Technology, Mid-Wales.

Far Right: A hay crop on the roof of a workshop in Herefordshire.

External wall finishes
Rigid sheets
Generally made from fibre-reinforced cement, impervious to water and with a high vapour resistance - so they will require ventilation behind for the wall to 'breathe'.

a) Colour glazed f.r.c. sheeting: expensive but long lasting and maintenance free (e.g. Glasal).

b) Plain f.r.c. sheeting: low cost, it can be painted (preferably with long lasting silicate paints) e.g. Minerit.

Boards
Timber boarding, a renewable material, whether horizontal (shiplap, feath-eredge) or vertical (board on board, board and batten) needs an air space behind to prevent water getting trapped. Needs regular maintenance or replacement.

Tiles

As with a pitched roof, a tile hung cladding gives a 'breathing' rain screen to the outside wall. Suitable tiles are: concrete, plain clay (high energy content), slate (tricky), or timber shingles or shakes.

Render

This is a mix of sand, cement and sometimes lime, used as a plaster on external walls. Rendering is a fairly skilled job. Fibre-reinforced render can be applied in two coats to woodwool slab for example. The fibres are polypropylene and are marketed as Krenit. Another product called Fibrocem uses glass fibres. The fibres act as a strengthener in the first coat of render, preventing cracking where there is a gap in the substrate, such as where woodwool slabs butt together. It yields a hard-wearing, low vapour resistance ('breathing') finish and can be left unpainted to show the natural sand colour, or painted with silicate paints.

Lime render is made by mixing slaked lime with coarse sand, and often in the past was 'bulked out' with animal hair and dung. It is undergoing a renewed popularity as its aesthetic properties and durability are redis-covered. It allows walls to 'breathe' and is particularly useful in retaining the characteristic look of traditional building.

Internal wall finishes
Plasterboard

The main constituent of plasterboard is gypsum, or calcium sulphate, which occurs naturally, is mined or quarried from the ground, and then heated to high temperatures. Gypsum also occurs as a by-product in the scrubbing of flue gases from power station emissions. This source is mildly radioactive and best avoided.

There is a new type of 'gypsum fibre board' just beginning to be imported into this country from Germany and the U.S.A. Made by blending recycled cellulose fibres with gypsum, it is stronger and more moisture-and-fire resistant than ordinary plasterboard. Coming with a plaster, rather than a paper, finish, it only needs the gaps between the boards to be filled to produce a surface ready for decorating. Although about twice the price of ordinary plasterboard, you would save on employing a plasterer to skim the boards (Fermacell and Fiberbond).

Top: Stained timber boarding at the first floor, f.r.c. coloured sheeting below, with concrete pantile roof on a Sea Saw Self Build house, Brighton.

Above: Dark-stained weatherboarding at the Hop Farm, Kent.

Top: Timber feather-edge board cladding and a roof finish of corrugated coloured f.r.c sheeting on a house in Telford, Shropshire.

Top Right: Timber cladding, tiled roof and conservatory on a house in Herefordshire.

Above: Timber cladding, turf roof on a studio house in Herefordshire.

Plasterboard and cover strips

These are relocatable, reusable components. The plasterboard is fitted loose and the timber cover strips cover the joins and hold it back against the studs. Installation is time-consuming careful work.

Plasterboard and filled joints

This system is not easily relocatable and some components will have to be scrapped on demolition. It is faster and costs less than the above, yielding better sound insulation. It can be done quite easily by a self builder and is the required finishing technique if using gypsum fibre board.

Plasterboard and skim

This option will incur the most cost as it is a very skilled job. It is messy too. But professional plasterers work surprisingly quickly and many self builders have found that this is a useful bit of the job to contract out.

Timber

This is a relatively quick and easy option, but expensive because of the material's cost. It does give an ideal 'breathing' and moisture absorbing finish.

Render

This is suitable for walls liable to get hard wear. Applying it is a fast but skilled job. Long drying out period required.

Floor finishes
Sheet materials

Virtually all wooden sheet materials - such as plywoods, chipboards, block-boards, oriented strand boards and medium density fibreboards - use adhesives to bond the sheets or fibres together. Formaldehyde-based glues, used in particularly large quantities in chipboard, can be harmful, especially in non-ventilated spaces or when burned. An irritant which can affect skin, eyes and nasal passages, formaldehyde has been classified by the World Health Organisation as a probable carcinogen. Douglas fir plywood is a low-formaldehyde product.

Timber boarding

This should be well seasoned, tightly clamped and finished with a microporous finish so that the timbers can 'breathe'. Second-hand boards of very attractive wood such as pitch pine or maple can be found by shopping around.

Above: Sand, lime and cement render on woodwool wall panels on housing in Churt, Surrey.

Below: The same combination of exterior wall finishing at the Centre for Alternative Technology Mid-Wales.

Thermal insulation

The table overleaf shows commonly available insulation materials, grouped according to their source. Renewable materials should be the first choice. The lower the conductivity, the better the insulator. On the whole it is better to have a thicker layer of less polluting (and probably cheaper) material, rather than a thinner layer of an exotic one.

Insulation effectiveness is indicated by a 'U'-value. This is a measure of heat flow, so the smaller the 'U'-value the better the insulation. For example a wall construction will consist of layers of materials of varying thickness and conductivity. All these added together will give us the 'U'-value, defined as heat flow through the wall (in Watts) per square metre of wall ($/m^2K$). Thus a single sheet of glass is rated at $6W/m^2K$ and two sheets at $3W/m^2K$ - halving the number of Watts escaping.

The following are examples of insulation materials and techniques currently used on Segal Method buildings.

Boards and slabs

These mostly have flat/low-pitch roof applications, particularly on 'upside-down' roofs, and in external walls.

a) Cork: expensive, but a renewable resource. Waterproof and long-lasting.

b) Foamed glass: expensive, but long lasting; energy consuming, but uses a plentiful resource.

c) Rigid, waterproof Rockwool: as the work is all done outside, the irritant properties of mineral wool are not so hazardous.

d) Expanded polystyrene sheet (Jablite): this is steam-blown, with no CFCs. A rigid, easily worked waterproof sheet available in different thicknesses. One drawback is that the little white beads get everywhere, and they don't biodegrade. All polystyrenes and polyurethanes are products of the highly polluting petro-chemical industry.

e) Extruded expanded polystyrene (e.g. Styrofoam, Polyfoam): lightweight, easy to use, low U-value. But, although the manufacturers claim that CFCs are no longer used in their production, they have usually substituted another CFC or HCFC. While the substitutes have a lower ozone depletion potential (ODP) than the original CFC-12, it is still significant, and they are also very potent

Above: *Timber ceiling and high-level under-eaves glazing, with a bay window and exposed structural timber; some of the delights of Segal Method building inside a studio house Herefordshire.*

greenhouse gases. In environmental terms, a very damaging material.

Sheathing and slab materials

a) Bitumen impregnated fibre-board: acts as an insulation retainer, structural sheathing and insulant. It is made from wood pulp and bitumen and can be tongued and grooved for roof sheathing (Bitvent, Frenit).

b) Woodwool: not a very good thermal insulator, but a rigid, cheap and relatively benign form of sheathing or infill panel. Being dense and heavy, it is a good absorber of sound. The sheets are reusable if they have not been nailed. It is produced by Torvale from small diameter logs of homegrown spruce or pine from (they tell us) sustainably managed forests. The wood shavings are coated with a cement slurry, then compressed into a mould-and-rot resistant slab. Care is taken to find uses for the by-products of this process. The bark is sold to garden centres; sawdust is used as animal bedding; and substandard and waste slabs go to make up horse training rings. There is also a product called Heraklith, manufactured in Austria but available in this country, similar to woodwool, but using naturally occurring magnesite as the binding agent, rather than cement.

Quilts

Mineral Wool: (e.g. Rockwool or glass fibre). Despite irritating effects, this is still being used where there is good ventilation. However it has been classified by the Environmental Protection Agency in the U.S.A. as a possible carcinogen. A dust mask and gloves are the minimum protective equipment which should be worn when installing this material.

Loose fill and sprayed fill

Cellulose Fibre: Most Segal Method builders are now using cellulose fibre insulation. It is made from recycled newsprint and treated against fire and vermin with borax. Marketed as Warmcel by a company with a good environmental record, it is a better insulant than mineral wool or expanded polystyrene and is particularly good at filling all potential draught gaps. When the building is demolished, it can be sucked out and used as a garden mulch.

Most self build groups have hired or invested in their own machine which breaks up and aerates the compressed bales, and then blows it down a long tube which delivers the material to wherever in the house it is needed. For horizontal spaces, such as under floors or in lofts, the Warmcel is simply blown in to the required depth. Alternatively, 'pre-fluffed' Warmcel can be poured straight in from the bag without needing a machine. Though it is more expensive to buy it this way, it is the only way you can do it yourself without hiring a machine. Some self build groups have invested in their own machine and have received training in its use. Vertical walls or sloping ceilings can be injected with Warmcel under pressure through a 1 inch diameter hole cut in the plasterboard and later filled. Alternatively, the Warmcel can be sprayed on to a vertical surface, before the plasterboard is fitted, using a fine mist of water to dampen

TYPE OF INSULATION MATERIAL	CONDUCTIVITY (λ) measured in Watts per m² per degree Celsius									
	.01	.02	.03	.04	.05	.06	.07	.08	.09	.10
ORGANIC: Derived from natural vegetation Renewable source Reclaimable upon demolition				φ CORK, slabs, tile and granular fill						
				φ EXPANDED RUBBER pipe sections, etc.						
					φ WOOD FIBRE insulation board					
								φ WOODWOOL rigid slabs		
				φ CELLULOSE loose fill in shredded paper pellet form						
INORGANIC: Derived from naturally occurring minerals Non-renewable but plentiful source Reclaimable upon demolition				φ MINERAL FIBRES rockwool, slagwool & fibreglass, quilts & rigid bats						
						φ PERLITE & VERMICULITE loose fill, aggregate for concrete				
										φ AERATED CONCRETE air-entrained in-situ concrete blocks
					φ FOAMED GLASS glass in cellular form					
SYNTHETIC ORGANIC: Derived by chemical industry from fossilised vegetation				φ EXPANDED POLYSTYRENE 'bead board' - usually white						
			φ EXTRUDED EXPANDED POLYSTYRENE semi-rigid smooth-skinned closed cell boards, usually tinted							
Difficult to reclaim upon demolition (check for use of CFCs or urea formaldehyde in manufacture)			φ POLYURETHANE FOAM closed cell semi-rigid boards and foam fill							
				φ UREA & PHENOL FORMALDEHYDE FOAM ditto						
			φ POLYISOCYANURATE FOAM ditto							

ELEMENT	U-VALUE (W/°C K)		APPROX INSULATION THICKNESS	
			mm	inches
Roof	0.17-0.12		250-300	10-12
Walls	0.22-0.17	Timber frame:	175-225	7-9
		Brick & block Cavity:	125-175	5-6
Floor	0.2	Suspended Timber:	150	6
		Solid concrete slab:	100	4
Windows	2.0		Double with Low-E glazing	
			Triple - 12mm airgaps between panes	

the fibres slightly and ctivate their natural tarch. This makes them tick to each other and to he structure, thus reventing settlement. oth of these applications eed a skilled operator ith the appropriate quipment, and in this case insulating has to happen in one operation.

ecorative finishes

: is very important to consider the internal climate of your house - not just how looks and functions, but how wholesome the air is to breathe, how friendly he surfaces are to touch. There is a whole school of thought, known as Building iology, dedicated to making the indoor environment as harmonious and alanced as possible, in order to mirror conditions found in nature. The fact that ick Building Syndrome is being taken increasingly seriously by employers, evelopers and users shows how important these concerns are.

Above Top: The effectiveness of different materials as insulators. The slashed circle shows where the material sits on the scale.
Below: Table showing insulation values to achieve 'superinsulation'.

Above: Damp-spraying Warmcel cellulose insulation into a timber stud wall (Top) and (Below) brushing off excess material to leave a flush finish for plasterboarding.

Floor coverings

Many floor coverings nowadays are synthetic, based on by-products of the petro-chemical industry, such as nylon, vinyl or P.V.C. They are relatively cheap, but the chemical additives they contain can affect the health of occupants.

Carpets

Carpets can be treated with up to 30 different chemicals, including insecticides and stain repellents. An untreated wool carpet is the best choice environmentally, and wears well, but is expensive. Look for a jute backing rather than plastic or synthetic rubber. Fitted carpets, which are almost universally popular, are in fact very difficult to clean thoroughly and can become infested with micro-organisms, including the house dust mite which can provoke allergic reactions. Consider using small carpets or rugs which can be aired and beaten.

Natural fibre matting

Many different types of fibre are available, all of them plant-based and therefore renewable, e.g. sisal, coir (coconut), seagrass and rush. An attractive and hard-wearing alternative to carpet.

Linoleum

Made from naturally occurring materials, (i.e. powdered cork, linseed oil, chalk, wood flour and resins), and bonded on to a hessian or jute backing, it is more expensive than vinyl or P.V.C., but it is strong, flexible and durable. It contains a natural anti-bacterial agent and is resistant to marks, knocks and burns (it does not melt). It should be laid on a clean dry surface with a lignin paste.

Cork

Another good ecological product, made from the bark of a particular South European oak that renews itself after being stripped. It is pressed into a sheet and then made into floor or wall tiles. These give excellent thermal and sound insulation. Hard-wearing, with an attractive natural grain, they can be laid with lignin paste, in preference to solvent-based adhesives. They will need sealing before use, preferably with an organic, microporous varnish. Avoid tiles that are vinyl-backed or pre-sealed with an acrylic varnish.

Gloss paints

These are generally solvent-based paints, used for external and internal joinery. The solvents, such as white spirit, toluene, xylene and benzene, give off chemicals known as Volatile Organic Compounds (VOCs) into the atmosphere. They continue to give off gas even when the paint is dry. The most toxic ingredient of paint, i.e. lead, has now been phased out in this country. Still, painting is a hazardous activity. Most painting in domestic situations is done in a very casual way, often without regard for the need to limit exposure and ventilate. In an industrial situation, by contrast, use of many of the common components of paint would involve controlled ventilation and air extraction, protective clothing and even breathing apparatus. All synthetic paints are especially dangerous in fires, emitting toxic gases and dense smoke.

These paints, together with the by-products of their manufacture, are non-biodegradable and are therefore potential contaminants. The manufacturing process is energy intensive, and produces a volume of chemical waste many times greater than the volume of the paint itself. The amount of VOCs produced by the paint industry almost equals the volume produced by car exhausts.

There is a new generation of water-based and low-solvent paints on the market, which are advertised as 'green' and are popular because of the absence of fumes. The building trade is turning increasingly to these paints as new Health and Safety regulations restrict the uncontrolled use of solvent-based paints. Although water-based paints are healthier and more pleasant to use, it seems that their manufacture causes even more environmental problems than those produced by the old solvent-based paints.

Microporous (or vapour-permeable) gloss paints are also available. These allow the timber to 'breathe' thereby preventing decay and rot.

Organic paints use natural, as opposed to synthetic, solvents such as gum turpentine and citrus peel oil. These solvents bond well with the oils and resins in wood, giving much better adhesion and protection. Organic paints are made from plant-derived raw materials in a low energy production process, whose few waste products will degrade naturally.

Emulsions

Emulsions are water-based paints for internal plastered or papered walls. Most contain vinyl which gives an impermeable, non-breathing finish. Organic alternatives are vinyl-free and contain no titanium dioxide, conventionally used to achieve the brilliant whiteness and opacity of white emulsion.

Varnishes and stains

Clear or coloured, these solvent-based coatings are used to protect wood from wear or weather, and are often used on floors as well as joinery. The solvents involved are basically the same as in gloss paints; the same warnings apply. Organic equivalents are resin oil-based with lead-free drying agents. They can be coloured with plant pigment dyes for weather protection, and enhanced with bee and plant waxes for inside finishes.

Silicate based paints

Used for external brick, stone, concrete or rendered walls. A high quality expensive product, very durable so therefore saving on the cost of maintenance. Made from natural ingredients, it gives a breathable surface, while forming a chemical bond with the substrate (e.g., Keim Paints).

Appendix: Tools

IN ADDITION TO a basic set of hand tools, there are several items which we have found invaluable on site:

Cordless drill

Once you have got one, you'll wonder how you ever managed without it. Quicker and safer than plug-in drills, it is ideal for pre-drilling holes for screws and nails, and for use as a screwdriver. For maximum convenience, get one with a keyless chuck and a spare battery pack. The bigger the rating (in volts), the greater the range of jobs it will do, although it's probably not worth trying to use it for masonry.

Electric drill

You will need a plug-in drill for drilling larger holes in timber, such as those which take the bolts, and for concrete, masonry or rendered surfaces. Most drills currently available have two gears and a hammer action. A variable speed on the on/off switch makes it easier to control. You will also need long (12"-18") augur bits the exact width of the bolts you are using. Because of their extra length you will have to order them specially. See the Resource Guide under Tewkesbury Saw Company.

Circular saw

Apart from an electric drill, a small, light circular saw is the one other power tool you are likely to use a great deal. Particularly useful for cutting sheet material, it can also be used for long, diagonal through cuts e.g. in scarf joints. It is extremely versatile and its adjustable depth of cut means that it can be used to form housing joints or tenons.

F cramps

Invaluable as a third hand for holding two pieces of wood together while you insert the fixings, or for securing wood to a trestle while you cut or drill it. They come with bars of varying lengths and the lower jaw screws up and down, giving the required gap. Final tightening of a screw plate in the lower jaw gives a firm hold. G cramps can be used for smaller section timbers.

Morticer

This is only necessary if you are planning to build traditionally jointed mortice and tenon frames.

It is a large but portable machine which clamps on to the timber being cut and, with a cutting chain, produces a clean, straight mortice up to 38mm wide, 100mm deep and virtually any length. It is expensive, but saves an infinite amount of time and trouble, as well as the cost of the bolts.

N.B. All power tools used on a building site should be rated at 110 volts. This may mean replacing some of your tools, but it is a standard safety requirement.

Scaffolding

It is not worth trying to economise on scaffolding. Due to its cost, there is often a temptation to use it round part of the building, or make do with a tower, when a full run is needed. However scaffolding should be seen as a necessary and integral cost of the whole building operation, not as an optional extra. Always have it erected by professionals.

For your own safety, scaffold any area where you are working above ground. If you are working in the middle of the building e.g. on rafters or joists, lay old boards or sheets temporarily on the joists below.

Scaffolding makes the job easier by providing a useful 'half way' storage space for such items as roofing materials or window frames. As a support for a block and tackle, it also provides a means of lifting heavy objects. If your frames are very large or top heavy, scaffolding can also serve as a useful winching point for raising them.

Appendix: Time and Money

How long will it take?

The length of time it will take to build your house depends on:

- Size and complexity of the building;
- Self-builder's skill and speed;
- How much time can be devoted;
- Whether any elements are subcontracted out.

Allow approximately 5 person days per square metre. For example, two people building their 80m²
house, full time (2 x 40 hour week) should allow
200 days - 33 calender weeks - 7.5 months. One
person building the same house part-time (say a
24 hour week) would take 133 calender weeks -
30 months - 2.5 years! Groups are currently
taking between twenty and twenty four months.

Time can be saved by spending money on
subcontracts - commonly, discrete areas of work
such as foundations, drainage, roofing, central
heating, electrics.

How much will it cost?

Building costs (excluding the cost of the land) can
be divided into two:

Materials costs

These will vary according to the size of the house,
as well as ground conditions, quality of finishes,
and so on. Generally the cost is in the range of
£300 - £350 per square metre of floor space. So,
the materials for an 80m² three-bedroomed house
will cost from about £24,000 to £28,000.

Charges, fees and set-up costs

- Charges for services (water, sewerage,
electricity, gas, telephone) will be around £2500
per house.
- Local Authority fees for Planning and Building
Regulations consents will cost around £500.
- For a full service, an architect will charge from
£3500 to £5000 depending on the number of
houses in a scheme, and thus the degree of
repetition.
- Site set-up costs (insurances, site accommodation, tools etc.) will be approximately £2500.

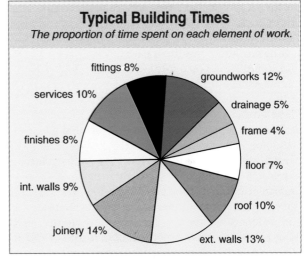

Typical Building Times
The proportion of time spent on each element of work.

fittings 8%
groundworks 12%
services 10%
drainage 5%
frame 4%
finishes 8%
floor 7%
int. walls 9%
roof 10%
joinery 14%
ext. walls 13%

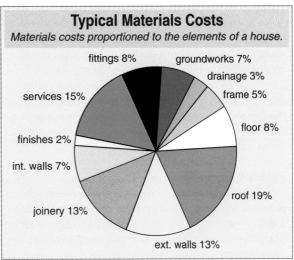

Typical Materials Costs
Materials costs proportioned to the elements of a house.

fittings 8%
groundworks 7%
drainage 3%
services 15%
frame 5%
floor 8%
finishes 2%
int. walls 7%
roof 19%
joinery 13%
ext. walls 13%

Appendix: Glossary

Terms unexplained elsewhere in this book:

Beam - A timber that spans between two points.
Biodegradability - Describes a material that can be broken down by biological action (fungi, bacteria) to its reusable constituent parts.
Birdsmouth - A notch formed in a rafter where it seats on its purlin.
Brace - An angled timber that triangulates a post and beam.
Bracing - Keeping pieces square by forming a triangle with another piece.
Greenfield sites - Land that hasn't previously been used for building.
In Situ - Built in its final position.
Joist - A horizontal timber that supports the floor or ceiling or flat roof.
kN - KiloNewtons, the metric unit of force.
kN.m - Kilo-Newton metres, the metric unit of bending moment.
Lath - Thin timbers that carry roof (or wall) finishes.
Loads - The weight of materials, people and snow and the force of the wind on a building.
Low-tech - A technology of simple, understandable materials and techniques that doesn't require highly sophisticated manufacturing processes.
Masonry - Walls or piers built of brick, concrete block or stone.
Module - A repeating dimension the same size as the building materials used.
Moment - Rotational force exerted on a beam.
Non-loadbearing - Taking no weight apart from its own.
Pier - Freestanding masonry block used to raise the building above the ground level.

Post - A vertical timber that supports beams.
Purlin - A horizontal roof beam.
Racking - The distortion by wind forces of a square frame into a parallelogram.
Radon gas - Naturally occurring radioactive gas given off from some granite rocks.
Rafter - A sloping roof beam.
Rain screen - The outermost waterproof layer of a construction usually spaced off from the main wall.
Risers - Vertical parts of a stair.
Scarf joint - Method of joining timbers end-to-end.
Services - Water, gas, oil heating or telephone supplies to a building and within a building.
Sheathing - Thin panels (e.g. plasterboard) fixed to timber studwalling to provide stiffness, containment of insulation and a finish.
Space heating - Heating the interior of a building.
Stud - A slender post used in wall framework.
'Stud' timber framing - Structural walls of small multiple posts, usually 600mm apart from each other, covered with sheet materials.
Superinsulation - Levels of insulation thickness required to create a very low-energy house.
Treads - Horizontal parts of a stair.

Resource Guide

Details of organisations, consultants, materials suppliers and publications concerned with Segal Method timber frame building and related ecological aspects of building.

The inclusion of any company does not constitute a recommendation for that company's products or services. Potential customers are advised to contact several companies to compare products, services and prices. A form is supplied for ordering most of the publications listed.

Organisations

ASSOCIATION FOR ENVIRONMENT-CONSCIOUS BUILDING
Nant-Y-Garreg, Saron, Llandysul, Camarthenshire SA44 5EJ.
Tel. 01559 370 908 Fax. same.
Offers advice on all aspects of 'green' building. Has produced a directory of environmentally-friendlier building products and services, which is available as a book or a database and a directory of members. Members get information on environmental building in a quarterly magazine, *Building for a Future.*

BUILDING CENTRE ENQUIRY SERVICE
Barbour Index, New Lodge, Drift Road, Windsor, Berkshire SL4 4RQ.
Tel. 01344 884999 Fax. 01344 884845.
Provides information on manufacturers and products for the building industry (contractors, architects, surveyors etc.)

BUILDING RESEARCH ENERGY CONSERVATION SUPPORT UNIT
Bucknalls Lane, Garston, Herts WD2 7JR.
Tel. 01923 894040 Fax. 01923 664097.
Centre for information, advice and promotion of energy efficiency in buildings. International R&D. Publications. DTI funded.

BUILDING RESEARCH ESTAB-LISHMENT Ltd.
Bucknalls Lane, Garston, Herts WD2 7JR.
Tel. 01923 894 040 Fax. 01923 664010.
Government funded research body. Produces 'BREEAM' (BRE Energy Assessment Management) for working out energy use in new homes, offices, etc. International research and development.

CENTRE FOR ALTERNATIVE TECHNOLOGY
Machynlleth, Powys SY20 9AZ.
Tel. 01654 702400 Fax. 01654 702782.
Visitor centre with displays on renewable energy and alternative housing, including

Walter Segal style, green oak and straw bale houses. Provides information, consultancy, public courses and publications on environmental building techniques. Mail order service. *Clean Slate* magazine available to members (free) and the public.

COED CYMRU
The Old Sawmill, Tregynon, Powys SY16 3PL.
Tel. 01686 650 777 Fax. 01686 650 696.
Provides advice on managing woods, hardwood product development, wood suppliers, manufacturers, architects, wood restoration.

ECOLOGICAL DESIGN ASSOCIATION
The British School, Slad Road, Stroud, Gloucestershire GL5 1QW.
Tel. 01453 765 575 Fax. 01453 759 211.
Educational charity promoting design for healthy and sustainable living. Directory of Members available which includes architects and building designers and a few timber frame specialists. Publishes *Ecodesign* magazine three times a year, and a newsletter six times a year for members.

ENERGY DESIGN ADVICE SCHEME
The Bartlett Graduate School, Philips House, UCL, Gower Street, London WC1E 6BT.
Tel. 0171 916 3891 Fax. 0171 916 3892.
Free one-day consultancy on energy matters for developers or architects and building owners of schemes over a certain size. Financed by the Department of Trade and Industry.

INSTITUTE OF BUILDING BIOLOGY
TARA, Rectory Lane, Ashdon, Nr. Saffron Walden, Essex CB10 2HN.
Tel. 01799 584727 Fax. 01799 584727.
Promotion of ecologically-sound buildings, a rapidly expanding development in Europe. Especially concerned with the quality of the indoor environment.

LONDON HAZARDS CENTRE
Interchange Studios, Dalby St. London NW5 3NQ.
Tel. 0171 267 3387 Fax. 0171 267 3397.
Charity providing information and advice on occupational and environmental hazards. Consultancy, publications and newsletter.
Deals with enquiries from organisations and associations rather than from individuals.

NATIONAL ENERGY FOUNDATION
No3 Benbow Court, Shenley Church End, Milton Keynes, Bucks MK5 6JG.
Tel. 01908 501908 Fax. 01908 504 848.
Independent charity promoting energy rating through the NHER - National Home Energy Rating Scheme. Also manages the South Midlands Energy Advice Centre network and is developing a National Energy Centre.

NATIONAL HOUSE BUILDING COUNCIL
Buildmark House, Chiltern Ave, Amersham, Bucks HP6 5AP.
Tel. 01494 434477 Fax. 01494 728521.
Runs its own certification scheme for new building methods. Mortgage lenders often rely on its recommendations. Good value National Home Energy Rating Scheme and SAP (an energy rating system).

SALVO
Ford Wood House, Berwick-Upon-Tweed, Northumberland TD15 2QF
Tel. 01668 216 494 Fax. 01668 216 494.
Promotes the use of reclaimed building materials. Publishes a newsletter and directory..

THE ECOLOGY BUILDING SOCIETY
18 Station Road, Cross Hills, Nr. Keighley, West Yorkshire BD20 7EH.
Tel. 01535 635933 Fax. 01535 636166.
Building society concerned with ecologically sound investments and purchases.

Organises mortgages, investments, conservation bonds, etc.

THE FOREST STEWARDSHIP COUNCIL
National Working Group Co-ordinator, Unit D, Old Station Building, Llanidloes, Powys SY18 6EB .
Tel. 01686 413916   Fax. 01686 412176.
A members association representing a diverse group of environmentalists, social groups, timber traders and foresters.

TIMBER RESEARCH AND DEVELOPMENT ASSOCIATION
Chiltern House, Stocking Lane, Hughenden Valley, Buckinghamshire HP14 4ND.
Tel. 01494 563091   Fax. 01494 565487.
Independent organisation providing R&D, information, technical services on all aspects of timber/products, i.e. testing, consultancy, training, site surveys.

WALTER SEGAL SELF BUILD TRUST
15 High Street, Belford, Northumberland NE70 7NG
Tel. 01668 213544   Fax. 01668 219247.
www.segalselfbuild.co.uk
A unique national charity with regional development workers which helps people, especially those with housing need and on low incomes, to build their own homes using the method, pioneered by architect Walter Segal, which makes such a task easy for the low-skilled individual or group. Provides a 'starter pack', which enables groups to get off the ground, and a membership magazine, *You Build*.

Consultants
BORER, PAT
Cwmwr Isaf, Penybontfawr, Montgomeryshire SY10 0HP.
Tel. 01691 860277   Fax. 01691 860277
Architect specialising in timber frame Segal style.

CENTRE FOR ALTERNATIVE TECHNOLOGY
See Organisations.

Services available from an hourly to a project by project basis, including feasibility studies.

ENERGY DESIGN ADVICE SCHEME
See Organisations.

HUTTON AND ROSTRON (ARCHITECTURAL SALVAGE INDEX)
Netley House, Gomshall, Surrey GU5 9QA.
Tel. 01483 203221   Fax. 01483 202911.
Experts in 'building pathology', diagnosing and treating timber decay, post-fire damage etc. Operate a data base of recyclable building materials.

Building Materials
Fixings
GALVANISED BOLTS AND NUTS
115 Lodgfield Rd, Halesowen, West Midlands B62 8AX.
Tel. 0121 602 3333   Fax. 0121 602 3222.

Supplier of virtually any size of bolt, washer, coach screw etc.

Flooring
CRUCIAL TRADING Co. Ltd.
The Market, Dale Street, Craven Arms, Shropshire SY7 9NF.
Tel. 01588 673666   Fax. 01588 673623.
Supplier of natural fibre floor coverings.

DLW FLOORINGS
Centurion Court, Milton Park, Abingdon, Oxfordshire OX14 4RY.
Tel. 01235 831296   Fax. 01235 861016.
Manufacturer of floor coverings.

F. BALL & CO Ltd.
Churnetside Business Park, Station Road, Cheddleton, Leek, Staffs ST13 7RS.
Tel. 01538 361633   Fax. 01538 361622.
Supplier of water-based, solvent-free contact adhesive for bonding many materials including rubber covings and textile floorings.

FORBO-NAIRN Ltd.
PO Box 1, Den Road, Kirkaldy, Fife KY1 2SB.
Tel. 01592 643777   Fax. 01592 643999.
Manufacturer of linoleum.

NATURAL WOOD FLOORING Co.
20 Smugglers Way, London SW18 1EQ.
Tel. 0181 871 9771   Fax. 0181 877 0273.
Supplier of wood floorings.

REIN
The Grange, Hall Drive, Clifton, Ashbourne, Derbyshire DE6 2GL.
Tel. 01335 342265   Fax. same as phone.
Manufactures Rein polypropeline fibres for reinforcing/improving variety of products made in cement and concrete - Krenit.

Insulation
ENERGY WAYS
Lordship Cottage, Barwick Road, Standon, Herts SG11 1PR.
Tel. 01920 821069   Fax. As phone.
Suppliers of Warmcell. Will install in the South East

EXCEL INDUSTRIES
13 Rassau Ind Estate, Ebbw Vale, Gwent NP3 5SD.
Tel. 01495 350655   Fax. 01495 350146.
Manufacturers of WARMCEL cellulose fibre insulation, made from recycled newspaper. Developed 'breathing' wall system. Good environmental record.

ROCKWOOL PRODUCTS Ltd.
Pencoed, Bridgend, CF35 6NY.
Tel. 01656 862621   Fax. 01656 862302.
Manufacturers of mineral fibre insulation.

VENCEL RESIL JABLITE Ltd.
Arndale House, 18-20 Spital St, Dartford, Kent DA1 2HT.
Tel. 01322 626600   Fax. 01322 626610.
Maker of CFC-free insulation; 'Jablite' expanded polystyrene board or granules insulation for roofing, floors and walls.

Kits
CARPENTER OAK AND WOODLAND COMPANY Ltd.
Hall Farm, Thickwood Lane, , Colerne, Chippenham, Wiltshire SN14 8BE.
Tel. 01225 743089   Fax. 01225 744100.
Supplier of kits for oak frame building, and designer of green oak houses.

CHRISTIAN TORSTEN
Unit B3, Wem Industrial Estate, Soulton Road, Wem, Shropshire SY4 5SD.
Tel. 01939 233416   Fax. 01939 234839.
Supplier of timber framed house kits and offers a full build service within a 40 mile radius of Wem.

Manufacturers
NURALITE UK Ltd.
Nuralite House, Canal Rd, Higham, Rochester, Kent ME3 7JA.
Tel. 01474 823451   Fax. 01474 823961.
Manufactures Nuralite FX, a bitumen-fibr product for flashings and gutter-linings. A long-lasting lead replacement. Preferable is the non-asbestos version.

ZEDCOR
Zedcor Business Park, Bridge St, Whitney, Oxon OX8 6LJ.
Tel. 01993 776346   Fax. 01993 776233.
Manufactures damp-proof membranes, made from recycled plastic, and damp-proof course.

Paint
AURO ORGANIC PAINT SUPPLIES Ltd.
Unit 1, Goldstones Farm, Ashdon, Saffron Walden, Essex CB10 2LZ.
Tel. 01799 584888   Fax. 01799 584042.
Suppliers of organic paints and full range of wood treatments. Use only naturally occuring ingredients in low-energy production process. No toxins.

KEIM PAINTS Ltd.
Muckley Cross, Morville, Nr. Bridgnorth, Shropshire WV16 4RR.
Tel. 01746 714543   Fax. 01746 714526.
Supplier of silicate based paints.

NUTSHELL NATURAL SUPPLIES
Hamlyn House, Mardle Way, Buckfastleigh, Devon TQ11 0NR.
Tel. 01364 642892   Fax. 01364 643888.
Manufactures and supplies environmentally friendly paints, pigments and wood treatments.

OSTERMANN AND SCHEIWE UK Ltd.
Osmo House, 26 Swakeleys Drive, Ickenham, Middlesex UB10 8QD.
Tel. 01895 234899   Fax. 01895 252171.
Distributerand supplier of natural wood finishes (clear, semi-transparent, opaque) for interior and exterior. Provides a specification service, free of charge, giving advice and guidance on wood finishings.

Roofing

DUNSTABLE RUBBER COMPANY Ltd. (D.R.C.)
Eastern Avenue Industrial Estate, Eastern Avenue, Dunstable, Bedfordshire LU5 4JY.
Tel. 01582 607718   Fax. 01582 471946.
Manufacturer of Hypalon, single membrane 'butyl' roof lining, and structural waterproofing.

ETERNIT UK Ltd.
Whaddon Road, Meldreth, Royston, Hertfordshire SG8 5RL.
Tel. 01763 260421   Fax. 01763 261331.
Manufacturer of fibre cement products, incl. slates, profiled sheeting, high performance claddings (external), fibre protection board and thin/solid laminates.

KALIKO ROOFING SYSTEMS
Unit 3, Bowlers Yard, High Street, Earls Barton, Northampton NN6 0JG.
Tel. 01604 812040   Fax. 01604 812019.
Supplier of 'Skylux' rooflights and 'Kalikuva' protection systems.

ONDULINE
Eardley House, 182-184 Campden Hill Road, Kensington, London W8 7AS.
Tel. 0171 727 0533   Fax. 0171 792 1390.
Bitumen and organic fibre corrugated roofing sheets - contains no asbestos - Onduline.

THE WORKS LANDSCAPE SERVICES
144 Wood Vale, Forest Hill, London SE23 3EB.
Tel. 0181 299 6997   Fax. As phone.
Undertakes design and building of turf roof constructions.

Sarking felt

KLOBER PLASTICS Ltd.
Pear Tree Industrial Est., Upper Langford, Avon BS18 7DJ.
Tel. 01934 853224   Fax. 01934 853221.
Supplier of sarking felts - 'Tyvek'- a 'breathing' membrane; also a range of roof windows.

Services

HEPWORTH PLASTICS
Hazlehead, Stocksbridge, S.Yorks S30 5HG.
Tel. 01226 763561   Fax. 01226 764827.
Manufactures the HEP 20 system of plastic plumbing for hot and cold water feeds.
NB: Hepworth Building Products is the department that deals with the HEP 20 system and not Hepworth Plastics. Also supplier of 'supersleve' clay piping system with polyethylene joints avoiding PVC.

NATURAL THERAPEUTICS
25 New Road, Spalding, Lincs PE11 1DQ.
Tel. 01775 761927   Fax. 01775 761104.
Supplier of demand switch circuit-breakers, for reducing electromagnetic radiation, and electro-stress relievers and mobile phone 'microwave' breakers.

WARM WORLD Ltd.
1 Hanham Business Park, Memorial Road, Hanham, Bristol, BS15 3JE.
Tel. 0117 949 8800   Fax. 0117 949 8888.
Manufactures 'Datatherm'-'intelligent' electronic controllers for heating systems. Supplier of ' Warm World' condensing boilers.

WILLAN BUILDING SERVICES Ltd.
2 Brooklands Road, Sale, Cheshire M33 3SS.
Tel. 0161 962 7113   Fax. 0161 905 2085.
Manufactures 'Passivent', a natural whole-house ventilation system using the stack effect to ensure air movement.

Timber

ALTHAM HARDWOOD CENTRE
Altham Corn Mill, Burnley Road, Altham, Accrington, Lancashire BB5 5UP.
Tel. 01282 771618   Fax. same.
Stocks conservation grade native timber for restoration of new buildings. Specialises in oak and elm. Offer construction/repair, machining. Also does joinery and site installation of oak beams and trusses.

CHARLES RANSFORD Ltd.
Station Street, Bishops Castle, Shrops. SY9 5AQ.
Tel. 01588 638331   Fax. 01588 638853.
Timber merchant and sawmiller involved with timber frame, supplying several self-build groups around London. Supplier of customised timber for frames.

ECOLOGICAL TRADING COMPANY
27 Lincoln Road, Fenton, Lincs LN1 2EP.
Tel. 01522 501 850   Fax. 01522 501841.

SAles tel/fax: 01427 719009.
Importer of sustainably-produced tropical hardwoods. Trades directly with the producers of the timber rather than the agents. Assists communities in the development of sustainable forestry projects aimed at a general improvement in living standards and care for the environment.

JAC BY THE STOWL Ltd.
Penrhiw House, Llanddeusant, SA19 9YW.
Tel. 01550 740306   Fax. 01550 740306.
A new company created to supply FSC (Forest Stewardship Council) accredited timber and timber products. Works with the FSC and the Soil Association's 'Woodmark' programme, coordinating a number of smaller and regional woodland enterprises. Hopes to supply every type of timber product. Can offer advice on woodland management.

JAMES LATHAM (NORTHERN) Ltd.
Longlands, Ossett, W. Yorkshire WF5 9JE.
Tel. 01924 276111   Fax. 01924 275156.
Supplier of a wide range of panel products, sustainably produced hardwoods, softwoods. Sawmilling and kilning service. Sustainably produced Brazilian mahogany authenticated by

Forests Forever.

MEDITE OF EUROPE Ltd.
10th Floor, Maitland House, Warrior Square, Southend on Sea, Essex SS1 2JY.
Tel. 01702 619044   Fax. 01702 617162.
Manufacturer of medium density fibreboard - a wood based panel made mainly from Lodgepole Pine and Sitka Spruce wood fibres bonded with synthetic resin.

MICK JONES
Cae Bardd, Guilsfield, Powys SY21 9DJ.
Tel. 01938 500283   Fax. 01938 500261.
Supplier of local oak, softwoods and flooring and maker of anything in wood to individual specifications.

MILLAND FINE TIMBER Ltd.
Iping Road, Milland, Hants GU30 7NA.
Tel. 01428 741505   Fax. 01428 741604.
Supplier of ecologically-sound hardwoods from properly managed forests in England, Europe, N.America and tropical zones.

NELSON, J.R.
The Sawmill, Newchurch, Kent TN29 0DT.
Tel. 01233 733309   Fax. 01233 733702.
Specialist sawyer and fabricator of seasoned timber - recycled pitch pine.

POWYS CASTLE ESTATES
Powys Castle Park, Welshpool, Powys SY21 8RG.
Tel. 01938 552554   Fax. 01938 556617.
Sawmill specialising in sawing oak, other homegrown hardwoods/softwoods - Larch/Douglas Fir.

PREN
Bryncroiau, Blaenpennal, Dyfed SY23 4TT.
Tel. 01974 251282   Fax. 01974 251282.
Specialises in local oak and related products, e.g. garden furniture and footbridges.

REMTOX
14 Spring Road, Smethwick, Warley,West Midlands B66 1PE.
Tel. 0121 525 5711   Fax. 0121 525 1740.
Supplier of boron rods and boron/glycol mixtures for treatment of timber against rot and insects.

Vapour control

BRITISH SISALKRAFT Ltd.
Commisioners Road, Strood, Kent ME2 4ED.
Tel. 01634 290505   Fax. 01634 291029.
Supplier of VCL Grade 411, the lowest vapour resistance available. Also Breather Paper Grade 234.

Walls

EASIWALL
Yaxley, Eye, Suffolk IP23 8BW.
Tel. 01379 783465   Fax. 01379 783659.
Supplier of 'Easiwall', consisting of stramit board wall partition system, which is a solid partitioning system of compressed straw. Easiwall conforms to BS 4046 and is fabricated using a patented process of heat

and pressure with no adhesives, making this a very natural partitioning board.

FALCON PANEL PRODUCTS
Unit C1A, The Dolphin Estate, Windmill Road West, Sunbury-On-Thames, TW16 7HE.
Tel. 01932 770123 Fax. 01932 783700..
Supplier of Hunton Sheathing 4D, a tongued and grooved, bitumen impregnated fibreboard and most other wooden pannelling products.

FILLCRETE Ltd.
Fillcrete Ltd., Grindell Street, Hull, HU9 1RT.
Tel. 01482 223405 Fax. 01482 327957.
Supplier of bitumen impregnated fibreboard 'Frenit' and Bitvent.

HERAKLITH Ltd.
21 Broadway, Maidenhead, Berkshire SL6 1NJ.
Tel. 01628 784330 Fax. 01628 74788.
Supplier of 'Heraklith' (woodwool/magnesite) board for sheathing and infill. Also offers a system-built timber-framed house using environmentally sound building materials.

L. SLACK & SON Ltd.
Glenview Works, Courthouse Street, Pontypridd, Mid Glamorgan CF37 1JX.
Tel. 01443 403301 Fax. 01443 407038.
Supplier of Minerit cladding/products plus a comprehensive range of specialist building products.

TORVALE BUILDING PRODUCTS
Pembridge, Leominster, Herefordshire HR6 9LA.
Tel. 01544 388262 Fax. 01544 388568.
Supplier of 'Woodwool' (shavings/cement) board, for sheathing or infill.

Windows
FORWOOD Ltd.
Joinery Sales, 13 Ashlyn Road, West Meadows Ind. Estate, Derbyshire DE21 6XE.
Tel. 01332 349161 Fax. 01332 291119.
Manufacturer of high performance, Scandinavian softwood, double and triple glazed windows and doors.

'O'WINDOWS U.K. Ltd.
Aylsham Road, Tuttington, Norfolk NR11 6TE.
Tel. 01263 735454 Fax. 01263 732781.
Manufacturer of high performance, Scandinavian softwood, double glazed windows and doors.

SASHY AND SASHY
46 Grosvenor Road, Tunbridge Wells, TN1 2AS.
Tel. 01892 514145 Fax. 01892 514221.
Scotland office: tel. 0131 660 2030.
Specialises in complete renovation and replacement of sash windows and doors.

SCANDINAVIAN JOINERY SYSTEMS

Monklands Industrial Estate, Kirkshaws Road, Coatbridge, Lanarkshire NL5 4RT.
Tel. 01236 427482 Fax. 01236 423910.
Manufacturer of high performance Scandinavian softwood, double and triple glazed windows and doors. Supplier of Nor-Dan products.

Publications

Out of the Woods: Ecological Designs for Timber Frame Self Build £12.50
Pat Borer and Cindy Harris. Foreword by David Bellamy 128pp. 1997
Building your own home is becoming increasingly popular and using this book you can also make the most environmentally friendly building possible. • The development of the Segal Method • From rough plans to your dream house • The ecological pros and cons of building materials - for any type of building • Where to obtain materials, help and other information • Profusely illustrated with 192 full colour plans and photographs of existing buildings. Published with the Walter Segal Self Build Trust

The Whole House Book £22.50
Pat Borer and Cindy Harris. Foreword by Richard Rogers 320pp. 1997
Whether you are renovating or extending an existing building, or starting from scratch, you will want to make sure it is comfortable to be in and has not cost the earth. • Building design for low energy consumption • Design for flexible living • Design for healthier habits • Design for ease of maintenance • The best material for each job. Full Colour Phone to confirm price. Approx. publication date: Nov. 1997

Environmental Building £1.20
P. Borer A4
The relative efficiencies of different heating sources; choosing materials; timber treatment; the site; low energy buildings; heat loss; 'breathing' walls; passive solar design; the death of a building.

Green Shift Symposium £6.50
Ed. Bryan Gould, 125pp. 1997
32 papers on green approaches to building design, taking a holistic approach and looking at many sides to the subject. Recommended for its thought-provoking ideas.

The Low Energy Self Build House at CAT £3.95
Description and plans of the Segal style tiber frame house, its construction and energy saving characteristics.

How to Build A Yurt £2.00
An experienced builder gives detailed illustrated DIY guide to these beautiful nomad's tents, made from coppiced wood. No experience necessary!

How to Build with Straw Bales £2.00
Straw bale houses can be timber framed or load supporting in themselves. This factsheet gives detailed DIY instructions.

Turf roofs £0.40
A detailed DIY guide with materials list and pros and cons.

How to Build a Tipi £0.30
Instructions for this North American mobile home, which is, of course, timber framed!

Environmental Building Resource Guide £1.50
Much bigger version of this guide to include all aspects of the subject.

Other Publications Available From C.A.T. Mail Order

Build a Classic Timber-Framed House £15.99
J.A.Sobon, Garden Way (1994) 202pp
Plans for an easily adaptable basic house design using timber frame construction Sobon's practical advice incorporates the latest knowledge on building a healthy house, integrating natural systems, and finding effective home heating solutions.

The Build It Guide to Managing the Build of Your Own Timber Frame Home £14.99
R.Renshaw, Dent (1993) 190pp
Inspiring, authoritative and full of useful advice, this book looks at every aspect of the subject and contains many photographs and clear drawings.

Building Your Own Home £19.99
M.Armour, Dent (1993) 286pp
How to get exactly the home you want. This covers all aspects from finding, evaluating and buying the site to designing the building, organising contracts and avoiding problems.

Eco-Renovation £9.95
E.Harland, Green Books (1995) 244pp
Shows how ecological thinking can be applied to planning a wide range of home improvements, thus conserving energy (and money) and helping the environment. Includes advice on choosing materials, organising space to the best effect and even using plants, plus information on locating products and services.

Green Architecture £18.95
Vale (1991) 192pp hardback
Packed full of ideas, examples and photos of energy efficient and aesthetically pleasing buildings. Very inspiring.

Greener Building £31.50
K.Hall and P.Warm, Association for Environment Conscious Building (1995)
Directory of products and services that have least impact on the environment. Analyses embodied energy levels and pollution in the manufacturing of common

building materials along side examples of approved ecological building products.

Low Cost Pole Building Construction
£11.99

R.Wolfe, Garden Way (1995) 182pp

This book will make the pole-building construction the answer to your building needs. Includes plans, examples and 'how-to'.

Monte Burch's Pole Building Projects
£14.99

Monte Burch, Garden Way (1995) 200pp

More than two dozen attractive, practical and useful pole building plans are presented from garden features upto full scale houses.

The Natural House Book
£12.99

D.Pearson, Gaia Books (1996) 288pp

This beautiful book is practical, inspiring and packed with ideas on how to create a healthy, harmonious and ecologically sound home. It concentrates on the aesthetic and health giving potential of buildings, within the context of global environmental concerns.

The Natural House Catalogue
£19.99

D.Pearson, Gaia Books (1996) 287pp

This book lists and includes details on the latest environmental technology, providing all the information you need to create and maintain your ideal living space.

A Pattern Language
£40.00

C.Alexander et al., OUP (1977) 1171pp

An inspirational aid in the design process, this book lists over 250 essential or desirable attributes of any building - past or present. These patterns can be combined to give a design which echoes the best building traditions world-wide, and which appeals to an innate aesthetic sense which we all share.

The Self-Build Book
£15.00

J.Broome and B.Richardson, Green Books (1995) 271pp

A definitive guide to the whole process from initial idea to completed project, complemented with a great range of built examples. Includes a detailed manual on the Segal method of timber construction. Also contains chapters on land, finance, permission and professional help.

Talking About Self Build
£7.50

R.Mattews, Blackberry Books (1990) 256pp

An invaluable collection of self-builders' own accounts of their projects. Highly personal, with all the delights and agonies encountered. Asked if she would do it again, one self-builder replied "Just give me the mud and the caravan". Includes a section on house-building packages and self-build consultants.

Simply Build Green
£9.95

J.Talbott, Findhorn (1995) 220pp

A fascinating description of one group's attempt to build an 'ecological village'. This was not a group of builders and they recorded the struggles and dilemmas of their learning experience with disarming openness. Nevertheless the author is technically proficient and the book contains authoritative information on all aspects of building, including an excellent description of how breathing walls are supposed to work.

Green Building Digest £23.00 for 4 issues

Bi-monthly magazine, building up over a year into an impressively researched and informative guide to the environmental impacts of different building materials. Available from ACTAC Ltd., Technical Aid Network, 64 Mount Pleasant Road, Liverpool, L3 5SD.

Products available from C.A.T. mail order:

Auro Natural Organic Paints

A healthier choice. Pleasant to use and aesthetically satisfying. Made from natural oils and resins - self-renewing resources.

Auro paints, waxes and varnishes are better for your health and kinder to the environment than are conventional paints. The natural chemistry employed in their manufacture produces neither toxic intermediate products nor environmentally damaging wastes. Lead, biocides and petroleum derivatives are strictly excluded from all formulations.

Emulsion and gloss paints, as well as artist's paints, are available in an attractive range of colours. There are waxes and varnishes for furniture, floors and wood stain systems for exterior protection. For those who are allergic to organic solvents (even natural ones) there is a new 6 colour range of outdoor/indoor, water based waxes.

If you order Auro products through the Centre you will get a 5% discount off the list of prices. Auro products are only available by mail order, contact Sabrina Wise on 01654-703409.; E-mail: orders@catmailorder.demon.co.uk.

Warmcell Insulation

A DIY insulation made from recycled newsprint, currently the most environmentally sensitive insulation you can buy. It is non toxic, non irritant and is safe to handle. It is also fire resistant consumes negligble energy in manufacture and contains no CFCs. It has thermal conductivity of 0.035 w/m C (comparable with mineral wool). Applications include loosefill loft insulation, vertical partitions and sloping ceilings. Warmcell may also be used for wall insulation of timber frame buildings.

Warmcell is only available by mail order. We do hold a few bags in stock for DIY solar panels, sold @ £12.00 each. If you are interested in further details please write to us or phone for a leaflet, which will explain how to measure your loft, and for an order form. Installation instructions and a free dust mask are included in all orders.

Afterword
by Brian Richardson

"**Y**OU'VE GOT THE words and music, now all you have to do is learn to croon," the sergeant told us; just one of the pearls of wisdom cast before us young recruits, still obliged to join the army immediately after the second world war.

Happily for me those days of national service are long past, and I now wholeheartedly repudiate all things military. Yet I learned many things then that have stayed with me and have merit in them.

One of these that impressed me was the clarity of the instruction we were given. The lecturer had a method. First he told us what he was about to tell us, then he told us it, then he told us what it was he had told us. So the messsage went in - we knew it. But even though the words had penetrated, we still "had to learn to croon", which I interpret as meaning that we only fully understand a task when we have actually attempted it.

The best way of learning is by doing.

It is my earnest hope that having absorbed the expert and lucid instruction found between these covers, on how to build out of the wood in post and beam, you will go at it with saw and screwdriver and learn by doing.

My belief, based on experience, is that you will learn fast, and that you will enjoy it.

It is this enjoyment of an important job well done that is the business of the Walter Segal Self Build Trust. We exist to spread it ever more widely and to give everybody the opportunity to apply their talents constructively in solving a problem that continues to baffle public authorities and private speculators alike - the provision of good housing.

What is 'good'? What is the quality we search for, but cannot name?

We cannot define it, but we know it. It is the house invested with our character, achieved by our effort; our place, our home.

Those of us who have had the opportunity to make it, feel very satisfied with it.

It is not easy work, but the huge, sometimes daunting task, involving weeks and months of strenuous effort, is relieved by the many pleasurable experiences that mark its progress.

One of the greatest moments in any self builder's life is when the patient and comparatively lonely work of making frames is done, and raising day comes.

For a few hours the site is thronged with eager helpers who arrive to find a flat pile of unrecognisable pieces of wood and depart at dusk leaving you with an entire outline-in-space of your long-dreamed-of structure. Recognisably your house.

That old saw, "many hands make light work", was another observation convincingly demonstrated to me while I was in the Royal Engineers, building by hand Bailey bridges of heavy steel components.

The secret lies in the timing.

It is astonishing to me still, how, by lifting together, an apparently monumental load can be effortlessly hoisted by a group of not especially strong people.

It is a sublime moment when, after the rhythmically delivered words of command that ensure perfect co-ordination have been given, your frame soars upwards.

Hands to - altogether, lift - HUP!

Brian Richardson, July 1994.

CAT Mail Order Form

For ordering items listed as being available from us, ONLY! Please check to avoid disappointment.
Please cut out or photocopy and send this form (with a continuation sheet if necessary) to:
Mail Order, CAT, Machynlleth, Powys SY20 9AZ. Please write in capitals.
A complete catalogue of environmental books and products, **'Buy Green By Mail'**,
is available on request for five first-class stamps.
You can phone orders to us (24 hours) on **01654 705959** or fax credit card orders on **01654 705999**.
email. mail.order@cat.org.uk **Website.** www.cat.org.uk

Title	Quantity	Price	Total
Cat Publications			
Other Publications			
Goods Total			
Add postage and packing (see chart below)			
Donation towards the work of CAT Charity (Thank You.) (charity number 265239)			
Membership of the Alternative Technology Association (£16.00)			
GRAND TOTAL			

U.K. postage and packaging rates as of January 2000 until further notice

◊ Goods total below £10   add £1.75
◊ Goods total £10.01-£20   add £3.50
◊ Goods total £20.01-£40   add £4.00
◊ Goods total over £40.00   add £4.50

Ordering overseas Postage & Packing
Europe, including Republic of Ireland - add 15% of total order for p+p. (minimum £2.00)
Rest of the world - add 30% of total order for p+p. (minimum £3.00)

Title ...... Initials .... Surname ....
Address ....
....
Postcode .... Tel. ....

I enclose a cheque/p.o. made out to CAT ❏
Please debit my Visa/Access/Mastercard/Connect/Switch ❏

Card number .... Signature ....
Expiry date .... Issue no. .... Date ....

CAT Publications: sustainable and environmental solutions

Also available from CAT Publications –

Order form on previous page. For a full list of publications send an A5 SAE

Architecture and Building

The Whole House Book – Ecological Building Design and Materials £35.00
Pat Borer & Cindy Harris
"...compulsory reading for every self-builder" – Self Build and Design Magazine

The Lemonade Stand – Exploring the unfamiliar by building large-scale models £19.95
Maurice Mitchell
"...a rich learning experience" – Reforesting Scotland

Environmental Building Resource Guide £3.00
Derived from CAT's huge, constantly updated database

Renewable Energy

Windpower Workshop – Building your own wind turbine £10.00
Hugh Piggott
"The author is a true guru of the art." – Positive News

It's a Breeze – A Guide to Choosing Windpower £5.99
Hugh Piggott, Advisor to 'Castaway 2000'

Off the Grid – Managing independent renewable energy systems £7.99
Paul Allen & Bob Todd

Tapping the Sun: A guide to solar water heating £3.50
Brian Horne, Pete Geddes

Solar Water Heating: A DIY Guide £5.99
Paul Trimby
"This book is a must" – Electronics and Beyond, The Maplin Magazine

Components of Renewable Energy Systems Resource Guide £2.00
Derived from CAT's huge, constantly updated database

Organic Growing

Creative Sustainable Gardening £12.99
Diana Anthony
"A colourful, easy-to-use, immensely practical book" – Gardens Made Easy

Ecological Sewage Treatment and Water Conservation

Lifting the Lid: An ecological approach to toilet systems £10.00
Peter Harper & Louise Halestrap
"...thorough, informed, authoritative and sometimes witty" – The Ecology Building Society

Sewage Solutions: Answering the call of nature £10.00
Nick Grant, Mark Moodie & Chris Weedon
" ...this book is a must" – Ecodesign